M000105916

PRISON SURVIVAL
HELL'S PRISM

MALLAH-DIVINE MALLAH

Copyright © 2018 Mallah-Divine Mallah
All rights reserved.

Book layout by www.ebooklaunch.com

Dedication

I dedicate this book to my Parents:

My father passed away on my third year in prison. He would never witness the man he wanted me to become. He saw the best in me regardless of the times I stumbled. He gave me a foundational structure of how a man should be. It was centered on accountability, respect, and being principle strong. Through me he still lives as I apply the lessons he taught.

A special dedication is due to my mother. She allowed me to parole to her house and live rent-free. She provided everything I needed to get started in my process of becoming whole again and integrating back into a human. She supported me going back to school and writing. She was open and patient with my development. I would not have published my first book *The Hidden Hand: Duality of Self* or obtain a Computer Network Technology degree if I didn't have a tranquil atmosphere to rest at. She saw my focus and determination and silently encouraged it. She is the angel watching over me.

Contents

Foreword by Dr Bernard Gassaway i

Introduction 1

Understanding Part One: Reflecting.......................... 3

My Journey Through Beelzebub's Playpen...................11

Prison Industry Complex......................................15

Prisoners 19

Family & Friends..26

Guerrilla Thinking and Urban Refinement...................28

Understanding Part Two:
A more personal look at my journey......................33

Next..37

Intake 47

Another Jail...54

Big House 67

Adjusting 75

Prison Life...82

Still living..86

Coming into my understanding.............................89

Off to the next...94

Nottoway..109

Back to the Yard 114

Mountain tour 128

Still in the Mts...136

Lunenburg 157

Living on LCC 168

Bloods 171

The tides started to change. 179

Last days 192

The Day 198

Refinement in Motion 201

Poem 9,984,960 Minutes...208

Survival Rules..209

The Hidden Hand: Duality of Self............................210

About the Author 211

About the Cover Artist...212

Final Request 213

Foreword by Dr Bernard Gassaway

Ava DuVernay's documentary *13th* chronicles how chattel slavery in America continued in the form of mass incarceration after the adoption of the 13th Amendment to the United States Constitution, which supposedly ended slavery in America. Former President Barack Obama opens the documentary by saying: "The United States is home to 5% of the world's population, but 25% of the world's prisoners." Mallah-Divine Mallah was once included in that astonishing statistic.

Prison Survival is his story. Mallah-Divine gives us a panoramic view of what goes on in the mind of a human being faced with the possibility of serving 55 years in prison for a murder conviction. His first-person account offers strategies or tools for men to combat the barbaric attempts of Department of Correction personnel to break the human spirit and soul.

As I read *Prison Survival*, I could not help but reflect that the best way to survive prison is to stay out of prison. Unfortunately, incarceration in America is a phenomenon that at least one in four Black men will face in a lifetime. This is largely based on a plethora of social ills, whether by design or happenstance, including poverty, poor education, poor housing, poor health, and lack of employment opportunities.

As a community stakeholder and public-school educator, I appreciate the vulnerability that Mallah-Divine had to reveal in order to share his story in a way that would benefit a cross-section of people, particularly Black men. Mallah-Divine, having spent nearly 20 years of his life in prison, offers an intimate look inside the physical and psychological world of incarceration.

Mallah-Divine gives a real and raw inside view of both the physical and mental prison that face a man being incarcerated in local jails and state prisons.

Mallah-Divine's chronological account of his 19 1/2-year human journey through prison does not glorify or glamorize life on the inside. He simply tells his story. He offers sound and insightful strategies that one might use to survive in a system that is designed to break one's soul and strip one of humanity.

Mallah-Divine tells of his struggle to maintain his sanity and humanity while "living" under some of the most inhuman conditions. He states, *"Being in prison is an exercise in trying to keep your sanity. But the biggest thing I had to keep was my humanity."*

I believe *Prison Survival* could be used as a significant credible resource for individuals, community-based organizations, and public institutions that work with youths. It could truly be transformational.

I have worked in public schools and in the area of youth development for over 30 years. As I read *Prison Survival*, I said, "This is another story that confirms the reality of the school-to-prison pipeline." It is true that there is a correlation between young men dropping out of school and dropping into prison.

I recently watched an HBO documentary entitled *Being Raised by the System*. In one hour, this documentary focused on the devastating reality of the effects of incarcerating juveniles in America. Basically, it portrayed the reality that children who are incarcerated are more likely to become incarcerated adults.

Mallah-Divine's unfiltered tale of what he experienced while in prison should be shared with adolescents. While Mallah-Divine does not shy away from describing some of the sexual predatory behaviors of men, I believe his story should be shared and taught in public schools, particularly high schools.

All health care professionals, particularly those who come in contact with children and families, should read *Prison Survival*. It should also be read by anyone associated with the American public-school systems.

I met brother Mallah-Divine at an event that he sponsored at the Borough of Manhattan Community College (BMCC), which he attended. While we did not exchange too many words, we made a connection that moved him to invite me to talk with student members of the Urban Male Leadership Academy, an entity designed to support men of color while in college.

I am so happy that Mallah-Divine was able to maintain his sanity and humanity. As a result, current and future generations of young Black men will be able to cultivate their brains and hopefully not only survive in prison, but also avoid prison by navigating the inevitable societal traps that feed our brightest boys and men to prisons, thus perpetuating the legacy of America's system of chattel slavery.

Much respect!

Dr Bernard Gassaway

Introduction

When I first envisioned this book, I wanted to have different incarcerated people's point-of-view. Brothers, I know that there are stand-up dudes in different state and federally pens. I wanted to create an opportunity for them to express themselves. I know they are credible messengers and don't glorify the prison experience. I also wanted them to have credit under their belt as being a published writer.

I had requested a 15,000-word essay from each of them. The mistake I made was I didn't consider that these men were not writers or had no inclination of being writers. I was more focus on putting out an authentic experience for the reader and went for the best people I had in mind.

In the end, some just did not want to be a part of the project. I respected their wishes. The brothers that did submit an essay one barely reached a 1000 words, and the other one came close with 8000. I will save both of those for a future project.

My essay for the initial project was titled *'My Journey Through Beelzebub's Playpen.* I kept it and just added it to my prison memoir.

Prison stories are often told in barbershops and on street corners amongst the people connected to the lifestyle. I want you to take a journey through my mind and experiences. It's almost 2.5 million people who are currently incarcerated and millions more on parole. Each one of them could have shared their stories, and some already have. What separates our stories is who the person is as a man or woman. What principles they stood on when they were in a weakened position. I chose to live by street codes at a young age. I paid the price and wondered if it was too high.

Understanding Part One: Reflecting

"Retrospection is the key for forward positive progression."
Mallah-Divine

I am sitting back thinking how did I get in such a wretched condition? Nobody told me what the fallout would be when I was older for being a thorough stand-up dude. I have been home for at least six months from doing almost 19 1/2 years in prison. That is around 9, 984,960 minutes of being amongst the half-dead: prisoners.

Yes, prison psychiatrist tries to fool us on the inside and you people in society with names like inmate or offender. Make no mistake I was a prisoner. My comrades are prisoners now and will be for the foreseeable future. The name game of those who are incarcerated is to try to control their minds. A master psychiatrist knows how words and colors play on a person psyche. If you identify yourself as a prisoner 6 out of 10 times, you will probably become socio-politically and culturally aware. If you think those who designed and still profit from the prison-industrial complex did not learn from the 1970's and 80's prison movements, then you are mistaken. The modern-day slave breakers have become more skillful in penology. They even turned a social responsibility into a profit-making scheme.

Look at the origin of police in this country. Check out paddy rollers during slavery. So, do not act surprised when you see more Black men in prison. No, they do not commit more crime. It was designed for freed hostages formally called slaves. A book called *Slavery by Another Name* documents how new laws were enacted to re-enslave the Black man after slavery. This was done up until WWII. How many broken homes were created with the stealing of the head of household?

Now, I as well as countless others are so-called free but if you on parole you are not. You are just doing your time under a zero-security level parameter. But you still feel the fetters and understand the power dynamic is not in your favor. Your moves are still limited. You must ask another person permission to travel, get your driving license, get a car, move residences, and have a curfew. Now imagine a grown man on a 7 am to 9 pm curfew; how am I supposed to date women if I got to come home before the streetlights come on? It's other things as well but, everything is at the discretion of your PO (and each one has his/her own style). But hey I am so-called free, so I should be tap dancing in the street with a watermelon smile.

Nobody had given me the *'game'* on the aftereffects of living a false street mentality. Honor, loyalty, and respect are great principles to live by. You just can't live by them in the streets. And if you do! You will be left holding the bag every time. Now if you are alright with doing football numbers or life in prison, then this book is not for you. It's for your newborn son when he reaches your age now. It's for your loved ones who need to understand what is ahead for them.

Prison is designed to dehumanize and humiliate you. But its primary task is to strap fetters on your mind and kill your spirit. There is no rehabilitation in there because that implies you were once habilitated to the status quo of society. And let me ask you when did African slaves who were Niggers/Negros then Colors and now Black/African-American become fully accepted and integrated into American society? Is it still a 3/5 clause in the Constitution? So, what can a Blackman be rehabilitated back into?

When did we play a part of the ideological development of the U.S. Constitution? The socially, politically, economically, and culturally systems were developed by WASPs (White Anglo-Saxon Protestants), Great Britain traitors, terrorists, or rebels; yesteryears Al-Qaeda or Boko Haram. So, at what point was these freed slaves habilitated? Was it during the Reconstruction Era or The Black Code Laws? Or was it during the time Martin Luther King was shot? Or is it now? I do not know. I am a formerly incarcerated person struggling to get a job and put the past behind me. But I can't because of the box (there or not) on the job application—have you ever been convicted of a felon? Or the question asked in an interview, *"Can you clear a background check?"*

I must put out a disclaimer now. It is hard for me, but I have family and friends unconditional support, so I am not drowning, homeless, or starving. I do not have to make hasty decisions about my survival. The good people around me know I am no slouch or complainer but a doer. It is just that some things take a moment to manifest. But everybody is not in my situation. Some formerly incarcerated people will make short-term choices with long-term consequences. I am not one of them.

I am like most people who came of age in the late 1980s to the early 1990's. It was a hardcore time in NYC. The era when the CIA introduced crack into the hood; Gary Webb's *Dark Alliance* proved this. But I had opportunities. I went to one of the best if not the best intermediate school in NYC called I.S. 383 (Philippa Schuyler School for the Gifted and Talent). When I left my third high school Francis Lewis, I had an 85-grade point average. Then I went on to a historically Black college called Norfolk State University (even though a year prior I was on Rikers Island). But every step of the way I would run into an invisible goal line stance and fumble the ball on the one-yard line.

I would get locked up for the first time at 17 years old for arm robbery. I always carried a hammer (gun) on me; it was like a credit card. I had fancied myself a stick-up kid rolling with a stick-up crew. I caught a break. My family got me a lawyer. I gotten sentenced to Youth Offender (YO) status and CASES. That was a good program.

But I never learned my lesson. I never changed my pattern of thinking. Most people like me are not taught to fear prison. You didn't welcome it, but you didn't fear it either. The sad thing is that I don't fear prison now. But I am not a criminal, so I do not worry about it.

My problem was like most young people now, especially Black youth. The exploitive nature of male on male bonding we grow up with in the hood. This existed before street crews, gangs, or street nations. Your crew or posse just reinforced this Illusionary concept of 'holding your man down.' You come up in urban cities your block is the center of your universe. Your friendship and brotherhood bonds are with your neighbors whose brothers, and cousins are all friends. So of course, if we are all tied together, older and younger brothers, as well as cousins running together our bonds are going to be super-tight. We are literally blood. On my block growing up, it had to be at least seven sets of brothers. I got an extreme set of values on friendship and brotherhood.

I did not know it then but would realize it after I was a captured pawn. That I valued being perceived as a stand-up dude more than I valued my own well-being and freedom. I figured I was insane. Some of the dangerous situations I would willingly be in, no sane person would swim in those waters. Could I have avoided a lot of predicaments I was in? Of course, but I did not care too.

Like most fools, I thought I was living honor, respect, and loyalty to the fullest. I was a dupe. Those pseudo values I would embrace came from a perceived reality of watching older cats get down. And the lore of Omerta (mafia codes). As well as the American reality of cowboyism, which is interwoven into the fabric of this society. The macho male bravado. All this was reinforced with accolades.

Being a stand-up dude was a choice for me or maybe an addiction. I think most males growing up on the planet want to be a stand-up dude or seen as a man of respect. A person that can be counted on in every situation. It's just the approach one uses that differ. See, you have to know your limitation on how far you are willing to go. I had no limitation, the only outcome for me was eventually getting judged by 12 in a box, which I preferred over being carried by six in a fancy box. I knew I would go to prison because I never value the laws of this country, especially when it interfered with my limited way of thinking.

Another reason is the level of police brutality I would witness coming up. I understood the police to be the enemy. That is what their actions showed me time and time again. This was decades before the Black Lives Matter Movement. I matured as a teen and started to develop the ability to rationalize the conditions going around me in the news. I realized this country was hostile to my existence. When I began to read historical literature on the Black experience, it validated my feelings from current reality and past events.

My catalyst for change was not after I was testified on in court. That was an eye-opener but not really a mentality changer. The first chink would come when my brother got locked back up, and the so-called victim in his case was another underworld mover, who would go to the police. But the death blow to my mask would be when one of my great friend's little brother wrote me from juvenile prison. Talking how he respect, admire me, as well as how I moved on the block *"like the street general."* That brought tears of remorse from my eyes that wouldn't drop. I realized that the next generation of young cats was watching my crew. Just like my crew watched the crew before us. I was a model for self-destruction. I knew right then and there I owed a community debt.

The hardest thing is to challenge a belief system that you thoroughly believed in, even after it failed you. So, at 21 years old I was in a transitional period in a hostile environment. I had one year in prison and became serious about the path I was just flirting with at the time. Some people might say that I went from the frying pan into the fire. I would embrace an unconventional set of transformative ideas under the Nation of Gods and Earths (NGE) tenets. Why? One reason I remembered how my uncle conducted himself around me. He was always clean, smelling of Blue Nile, and manifested a radical image of a Black man. He had his own flaws and struggles, but that was his battle. And second a lot of the values of the NGE, I already lived by in some shape or fashion.

I would become the living embodiment of the teachings of the NGE. I would use each degree as a key to discover another element about my mind frame. I would use them as a roadmap to discover the gems of life. I was on the operation table, and these teachings were part of a plasma transfer I was receiving. I was centrifuging false values and ideas out of my cerebrum membranes.

Being in prison is an exercise in trying to keep your sanity. But the biggest thing I had to keep was my humanity. Any man that walks out of prison sane and human committed himself early in his bid to be some type of fighter against the system. I had to despise everything about incarceration. I had to let disdain fuel me. Because the first time you get complacent, you will compromise. And it is nothing like seeing men you once respected break.

Some break for the promise of early release. I watched an ex-partner of mine who was a hell-raiser gangster type fold. He had organized a group of prisoners to disobey a new unjust grooming policy. They went to hole[1]and back there fought the Correctional Officers (CO's). One of those demons hit him with the stun gun in his gonads. The administration knew he was the leader. They offered him all his good time back if he would just cut his hair and come out the hole. He did. How do I know? Because he told me! I immediately lost respect for him, because he led those brothers who had anywhere from 15-30 years to do down the abyss. He was a weak leader. The worst kind produced

---

[1] . It is the jail within a prison.

in the Black experience. He leveraged his people for his own benefit. While he would be going home in 5 months after he surrendered who he used to be. He eventually caught a Federal life sentence. His right-hand man who he told me was his brother snitched on him. I hope you just paid attention to what I just stated.

But people break, and that's a fact of life in a despicable environment. I have seen more men fall apart because of loneliness than anything else. The psychological warfare that goes on is like nothing I have ever seen before. Why? Because you don't know it exist until you enter the Terror Dome. Two personality types (strong and weak) enter but only one will leave. You might come out with a female name identifying yourself as a woman.

Those that brag about prison are usually the lames that came home. NO, true man would want anybody to go through such a dehumanizing experience. Where you have to exist on super alert status; even while you are sleeping. And the strength you gain come at an emotional loss. Those that truly survive and strive on a bid shut down almost all aspects of their emotions, especially the ones that tie them to their loved ones. Why? No man can live in two worlds at the same time. And not being fully invested mentally in prison at every moment can cost you your life.

After coming home from a stretch

Coming home after 19 1/2 years was a welcome experience. But nobody had prepared me because you can't prepare for the unknown. My support level was stronger than average.

My struggle came with discarding a set of ideological tools from beyond the wall. Even though I have lived half my life by them. I realized I was off balanced when I was in the gym working out and a person passed by my head too close. This would never happen in the pen. My first reaction was to check this person, but the reflection in the mirror looking back allowed me to look at myself. I knew with all the discipline I had; I still had to develop a new way of thinking out here in the society.

New York City (NYC) is one of the rudest cities on the planet. But being a formerly incarcerated person, if you smack one of these good citizens regardless of what they have done—you lose. I realized I as well had a space problem. I was uncomfortable with strangers inside my two feet radius. I was wise enough to negotiate a different understanding with myself. The most important thing is freedom and being on parole it is tentative. That was branded on my brain.

Parole is different for everybody. If you go in there trying to run a con on your Parole Officer (PO), not respecting that they have seen and heard all the bullshit before you, and probably from better actors. All you did was just created a bad impression. If you go in there like you are dealing with a CO and not speaking with this so-called convict state of mind you are going to have a tough time and eventually have steel back on your wrist. What I can interpret is PO's want a person they don't have to worry about. If you are into bettering yourself and taking steps to show it, then you will be alright. Some PO's are ass-holes because I heard the stories and seen a few of their behavior, but that's not my experience.

I am going to do my best to share my experiences with you. It took a lot for me to write a memoir of my story because most of the stuff I am trying to forget. I take no pride in having been to prison nor am I embarrassed by it.

As I open myself up to you. I hope you realize prison is not a rite of passage. It's a descent into hell. Its Beelzebub's playpen. The wisest person learns from somebody else experiences.

My Journey Through Beelzebub's Playpen

No man or woman who enters prison comes out unscathed, whether mentally, physically, emotionally, or spiritually.

Mentally

If you do not actively train or engage your mind with practical, productive, and progressive ideas; it will deteriorate. You will see this at its apex in the hole. You will witness a man throw feces mixed with spoil milk or urine on a CO or fellow prisoner. What level of mentality does another human have to sink to, to save his own body waste and weaponized it?

The prison experience itself is designed to humiliate you and break you. But your mind must be broken first.

Physically

It is a real possibility that you can be maimed or killed in this environment. Killers have left prison in body bags. This is not a safe haven for anyone. Another way your health can be compromised is by catching TB, HIV, hepatitis, chicken pox, MRSA, diabetes. As well as a large portion of prisoners suffer from high blood pressure and cholesterol from all the process food they feed you and junk food sold through commissary. I also have seen a few prisoners with their limbs cut off. But the *worst* assault that can be done to your body is rape.

Emotionally

You have to shut off any emotional feelings that you would normally reserve for a woman. And the longer your bid, the more extreme you have to fight that feeling of loneliness (and accept being alone). You have to master the initial onslaught of bitterness you will feel when family and friends start to lie (maybe not intentionally), fall off in their commits to you, or just disappear. If you do not master your emotions, it will turn into hate. You will become a toxic individual or even worse a predator.

The things you will see that you *'do not see'* will tax your empathy and sympathy, because you will see *'do not see'* things routinely. They become a part of the atmosphere itself. You will become emotionally conditioned to not respond with compassion and accept violence as easy as you would accept a slice of American apple pie.

Spiritually

If you do not practice balance with your religious or spiritual discipline, you will fall into extremism, and detach yourself from the realm of reality. I have seen people forfeit all their legal preparation and leaving it in Allah or God's hands. You should be doing everything to get yourself back out into the free world. The lack of balance will leave you ill-prepared to excel in society once your bid is over. You can and will get lost in religion addiction. If you do not have balance.

Prison is designed to attack these four aspects of yourself. This is the prison industrial complex, and you are a commodity, it's to the benefit of those who get rich off of social misery to keep you weak, blind, death, and dumb. American Correctional Association (the policymakers and profiteers) research continues to come up with strategies to do this. They need docile cattle to get their capital and no outside eyes on their operation. They know nobody cares about the fallen.

The Experience

Prison is designed to dehumanize you. The first thing they do is strip you of your name and assign you a number like livestock, which they count at least 4 times a day. This identification number has to be on everything you sign, including outgoing and incoming mail. Another aspect of this dehumanization is changing what the Department of Correction (DOC) designate to call you: "prisoner", "inmate", "offender"; unless you escape than they use "escaped prisoner" or "convict". They are very skilled in the manipulation of words and the feelings that words conjure up and images it produces.

Your whole life is regulated from the time you go to eat, what you eat, where you sleep, what you wear, and when you get recreation (rec). The VADOC even regulates what you read and listen to. If they don't approve it, you won't have it—free choice is severely limited. You can only get visits and call people from an approved list that is limited to 15 people. Phones calls are monitored, and collect calls are extremely high[2]. They will block your numbers trying to get your peoples to switch their phone company. All this is done to break your spirit and limit your access to the free world.

The limitation of access to the free world and ideas is vital in the control process. It's a low-level form of brainwashing. If the VADOC can control the diameter of your thinking, it is reasonable to conduce your responses to favor what is perceived as *"orderly conduct."* This is some modern-day MK ULTRA program.

A large part of the prison staff are mental midgets, who lack education, and some are even criminals. They will use extreme brutality in a cowardly fashion usually done when you are in handcuffs. All of the prison staff works together, and segments of the CO's are in criminal cohorts with certain prisoners in the drug and cell-phone trade. One plantation even had a CO prostitution ring. What do you think going to happen when you owe money? It has been incidents when cell doors are mysteriously popped open and prisoners(s) rundown on another one. The CO on post covertly disappears or conveniently does not see the assault. They cover each other when they are wrong—making the grievance process obsolete on the institutional level. Unless you can show a constitutional violation and willing to file a civil suit called 1983; which is anywhere between 350-450

---

[2] The phone system has changed in the VADOC from when I was there. The rates are cheaper.

dollars. You are going to have to bite the bullet on some humiliation or discriminations. If you can, be sure to get this book **Jailhouse Lawyer's Handbook**[3]

The more you grow socio-politically and start to cultivate your ideas by ordering progressive books, magazines, or any publications to help your development it will get disapproved at the intuitional level. They will claim that it is on the ban book list or should be reviewed to be on it. Once you challenge it, it gets sent up the chain to a rubber stamp Publication Review Publication Committee. The crazy thing is the CO's find a lot of books on the Black American experience as being detrimental to your rehabilitation process. Especially if it's progressive or radical (in their eyes). They even had The *Autobiography of Malcolm X* on this list. This is after America made him into a postage stamp.

If you are used to eating gourmet, wholesome, or just fast-food, be in for a rude awakening! The quality of prison food is dismally poor, and the portion you will receive will keep a small child hungry. The mental midgets claim the meals are based off a 2000 calories diet and yes, they even count the butter.

---

[3] **Jailhouse Lawyer's Handbook**, The National Lawyers Guild, National Office [132] Nassau Street, Room 922 New York, NY 10038

Prison Industry Complex

"The United States is Fast Becoming One of the Biggest Open-Air Prisons on Earth" Mumia Abu-Jamal

It is set up just like slavery—the commoditizing of humans (mainly of African & so-called Hispanics/Latinos)

From a historical context of slavery and paddy rollers, you can see where police, prison guards (correctional officers), the convict leasing system, and the modern so-called correctional system arrived from.

A bigger game is being played here. The politicians and businessmen are cronies in this billion-dollar industry.

Your interactions with most staff are unequal. In their mind, you are beneath them because of your lost social status. Even though, most CO's come from the poorest character of humans and minimal educational background. The power for them to disenfranchise a prisoner is real. They master lies. These lies can affect when you go home and your living condition there: with the loss of so-called privileges, you are placed in the hole, and/or your security level risen.

Some prisoners rob or sneak thief (this is a no, no) from other prisoners because they have no money to buy commissary. The commissary is where prisoners buy snacks, hygiene products, and minor medical supplies at extortion rate prices. Which has become a big business for companies like Keefe Commissary Network (KCN) which claim to be the nation's leading provider of automated commissary management services and technologies to city, county, and state correctional facilities nationwide. They market a lot of their own products at unreasonable prices. They are in about 17 states. According to an article in Vice. Com called *I am Busted*, Seth Ferranti, he writes, *"The Keefe Company, is owned by the Bush Family."* That is something if you consider that two brothers were Governor and one became President during the rise of the prison explosion on the state and federal level.

From my own experience before Keefe, you could go to commissary and spend $40 and have a commissary that lasted at least a month. The commissary prices never went up under local vendors, and this was for my first 10 years in prison. After Keefe came into the Virginia Correctional System. You could spend $100, and it will not last a month. As well as, they raised their prices every 3 months. When you consider a prisoner's jobs only pay like .20-.85 cents per hour, where do you think the money comes from that Keefe slurps up? Our family.

Another racket going on in prison is the telephone system—which charges exorbitant rates for a 15-minute call. You might pay anywhere from $7-20 for a call, and if you have family out-of-state calls will be around $15-$20. This is another tactic to isolate you from your love ones. They understand most prisoners come from impoverished or working-class families. Companies like Global Tel give a 40% kickback to the D.O.Cs. You have to ask yourself, how is this allowed?

The creation of money schemes by prison officials, politicians, and businessmen is an ongoing process. They conjured up the outsourcing of how your family sends you money. Before families and friends would just mail you a money order, now they have to use Jpay[4] wire service and pay a fee. Your family can still mail money, but it must go to Jpay in Florida, which might take 2 weeks to post on your account in another state. They know you are going to discourage your family from doing this because you can only go to the commissary on certain days.

It is interesting the connection between politician and businesses that provide so-called services to prison. A stimulating read would be *Why are there so many black men in prison?* by Demico Boothe.

---

[4] JPay is a privately held corrections-related service provider based in the United States with its headquarters in Miramar, Florida

The medical department

Medical practices in prison is not designed to keep you alive. The remedy for most sick call visits is the standard prison special: generic aspirins, muscle rub, and Ace bandage. One time my foot swelled up looking like the elephant man, which I had to drag. I would go to medical, and they gave me the prison special. They brushed it off as a sprain without doing an exam. I told them this was not a sprain I had a sprain before. The nurse was dismissive of me. I wonder how compassionless people can work in the medical field. Then it hit me. They don't see a prisoner as a human. I had to weight my option on how far I was going to push this issue at the moment. I knew this was not worth going to the hole over. I was getting better at strategic laydowns. I kept pushing paper through the grievance process. Months later, I was sent out of prison to see a specialist who diagnosed me with a slightly torn Achilles tendon.

Another prisoner was a day or two from going home and went to medical and complained about his stomach. They gave him generic Maalox. He kept complaining when they finally took him seriously; he was hours away from dying from a burst appendix.

An elder associate of mines named Shaft who turned me on to the concept of Pan-Africanism died during a lockdown[5]. He complained for days that he couldn't move his bowels. When they finally took him to medical he never came back. He died because his liver wasn't working right.

These imps are the lowest in their profession. A prisoner *"accidentally"* had acid poured into his ear causing him to lose a percentage of his hearing in one ear. How unobservant do you have to be to pour acid in a person's ear? INCOMPETENT!

On one plantation camp I was on, in one year, five prisoners had heart attacks. The ones that died were all African-Americans. One complaint about chest pain. The *"wise"* people

---

[5] All normal procedures are stopped, and we are locked in our cells for a day to two weeks.

sent him back to his cell, which is against protocol when you complain about chest pain. He would die later that night. Is this part of some diabolic plan: maim or kill as many prisoners as you possibly can?

Even the dentist gets in on this fucking you up action. One time a dentist broke a prisoner's jaw trying to extract a tooth. His sausage fingers were so heavy and unskilled in your mouth you spit bloody flesh bits after a teeth cleaning.

You can see from these morbid tales the value of your life is less than the value of the animals PETA activist takes a pro-active stance for. A dog has more human rights than a man (ask Michael Vick) once you enter the house of oppression.

The pill line is longer than the Chow[6] line. The prisoners in the line are all not getting high blood pressure, diabetes or cholesterol medication. A percentage of them are getting medication to treat their fractured sanity. A lot of these fellas need to be in mental institutions. I've been on plantations[7] where they have mental health pods. I guess it's cheaper to throw them in prison that neutralizes the rehabilitation argument. How can you reintegrate a mentally incompetent man back into society?

But prison itself will deteriorate some people's mind. The prison places so-called violent prisoners on drugs to make them zombies. Some of the most thorough dudes get tricked into taking all sort of medication. They get dependent on them and go crazy when their medication is not on time. This happens too frequently to be coincidental. My take is they are running experiments on these dudes. It's a sad sight to see.

The break from reality happens too often. You will never know how you will response in this type of environment. It is a real-life *The Twilight* Zone.[8]

---

[6] . Chow is the name for meal call.

[7] Another name for a prison.

[8] A sci-fiction TV series.

Prisoners

"Poor people, people of color - especially are much more likely to be found in prison than in institutions of higher education."
Angela Davis

When you are a new jack[9] in prison, perceived weak, preda-tory animals with human make-up will hunt you. I have had my ears polluted hearing inmates brag in the common area on how they talked another man out their boxers or had him suck their dick. Other predators use the store-box[10], drug game, and/or gambling angle to get an inmate into debt. Then they intimidate the scared fella with a banger;[11] and tell him *"to bleed on this dick or this knife."* Some just go straight savage and rape them. These animalistic barbarians are the lowest and worst kind of pseudo-

---

[9] A term used to describe a first timer to the system.
[10] An underground commissary store a prisoner runs and charge a tax on the items you borrow.
[11] A homemade knife.

humans. They usually target the youth and/or Caucasians, who are not willing to maim or kill to protect themselves.

One time this bottom feeder was bragging how he turned out his latest boy (punk).[12] A Caucasian he named Valley boy. He named all his victims that name. I was curious why, but I never asked him because I knew he would have told me. I didn't want to hear his sick philosophy. I was in front of my cell observing how he had a few dudes' attention. They were viewing him like he was some type of pimp. We just were coming off a lockdown. He continued to brag, *"I told him only punks and homosexuals could move in my cell."* Since this was a new jack and the institution was on lockdown, he didn't know the protocol: Do not unpack your stuff and bang on the door to get out of the cell or fight to the death. So, the animal with the veneer of human cosmetics on beat the new jack-up raped him, made him douche his anal with a shampoo bottle, raped him again, and renamed him Valley boy. Then the savage ended off the story saying, *"I know he has been fucked before because I didn't have shit on my dick."* This cat was truly sick. Word was he died from AIDS a decade later. How many Valley Boys would he infect along the way?

Prison has turned into a homosexual making factory, especial nowadays, with the growing strength of the LGBT Movement. Different crews have gone to war behind a homosexual. These punks get into catfights, and then their so-called men get involved. The result is bloodshed.

One of my homeboys[13], who was a getting money punk, would seduce the young males for sexual favors with weed. But he was a flip artist. Punks of his master ability usually wind up fucking the young males turning them into his bitch. At their core, they are extreme predators.

Homosexual lover spats always turn violent. The punks are skilled manipulators and head game players. They want to feel

---

[12] The term giving to the male who is the supposedly female in a homosexual relationship.

[13] A person for the same city you are from.

like a real woman, so they keep soap opera type nonsense going on. This is some sad shit to see. A so-called man losing his cool over a punk—who he probably treated better than any female he had when he was free.

When you see dudes that supposed to be stand-up dudes and/or live by the tenets of the Nation of Gods and Earths, Rastafarian, Muslims, Street Nations, or any group that doesn't accept homosexuality, and he gets caught dealing with that—creeping. The situations get even worst when the dude tries to keep his illicit affair on the down-low, and the punk put him on blast on the yard. This is done to humiliate and isolate him. Depending on the group the down-low brother is affiliated with, it's going to be punitive repercussion and/or banishment.

A lot of dudes who enter prison and get into that homosexual current lose a lot of respect from stand-up dudes. Why? Because no real man would lower his standard and dishonor himself. Pain and loneliness are part of the bid. If you are not prepared for it, then stay out the streets. Always keep in mind punks are extremely dangerous and highly skilled in mind manipulation. They are superb predators appearing to play a weaker role with feminine attributes!

The Mind

At times prisoners psyche breakdown. Time affects everyone differently. One day a fella just decides to go in his cell, grab his comb, and take out one of his eyeballs. Another one who thought he was a woman kept trying to cut off his penis. I have witnessed many incidents where prisoners just have conversations with themselves: one prisoner was off his meds and talking aggressively to nobody in particular but in a dorm. Another prisoner took an offense and around 1 o'clock in the morning attacked him while he was sleep. A segment of prisoners are probably legally insane, so you never know what will offend a person—this plays a part in the level of prison violence.

At times, you will have prisoners screaming repress memories at 2 or 3 in the morning. They always sound like they were victims of sexual molestation when they were children. Prison is a warehouse of sad stories and shattered dreams.

The minds of some prisoners over time allows them to develop and rationalize abnormal behavior. One fella had to be rushed to the hospital because he had the roll-on ball from a deodorant stuck in his ass. Another one got caught sucking his own dick and get the moniker *"Rubberneck."*

A few prisoners have mastered the art of conning other prisoners out of their resources. They watch and see who have money coming in or who gets the pack/sack[14]. They form parasitical type relationship with them. The worst vampire leeches are those who pose like they know the law. They set up traps in the law library playing on a prisoners' desperation. They know especially since Bill Clinton so-called first Black president (real Blackman take that as an insult) signed the **1996 Anti-Terrorism Bill** into the law. It leaves prisoners with a one-year time limit to file their Federal Habeas Corpus—their last chance at freedom. This scum tick plays on a person's need to gain legal weaponry to resurface in his legal battle, after receiving poor representation from an agent of the damn (lawyer). Some brilliant stand-up prisoners know the law and do better work than lawyers. So be wise when you seek help in the law library.

Respect is a slippery slope in prison. Why? Because prison is designed to humiliate you by those who are so-called in power. They regulate you unnecessarily. Most of the people enforcing the rules are a level above idiots, so they abuse their authority. All a prisoner has left is perceived manhood. It will determine his value system.

You have to be on hyper-alert all the time. Violence jumps off anyplace for any reason. Be aware of who you walk with. If he gets in something, you inherit the outcome as well. There are no choosing sides or sitting it out once the violence erupts.

---

[14] The term for the drug package.

Things can get crazy in what a prisoner place value on. When you have little, it becomes a treasure. On one plantation, a prisoner stabbed another one over a porno magazine that he borrowed and never gave back. The sad thing is the prisoner whose magazine it was, was going back to court to challenge his 300-year sentence. But that porno magazine meant more.

There is a fainthearted level predator called a sneak thief— he breaks into a prisoner's cell/lockers and steals their property when nobody is around. Masters locks are child's play to these chief cowards. When all else fail they will just peel your locker back like a sardine can. These crawlers are dangerous because you don't know who they are at first. It's usually a lame doing this because no self-respecting man or gangster slithers to that type of low. When they are discovered the whole pod/cell-block or dorm turns on them. A sneak thief is looked upon as a man with no honor. The flipside is it is perfectly acceptable for someone to come take your stuff in front of you. Either you fight for it or you lose it.

Fights start with the least bit of provocation. A misunderstanding. A look. A word said out of place, taken out of context, in the wrong tone, or in a disrespectful manner (or perceived as being disrespectful) going cause some violent act to jump off. The main culprits are the phone, card games, sports, basically different opinions about anything. You have had prisoners fight over who was the better M.C., Biggie or Tupac. You have to be willing to defend yourself at all times. Depending on who your opposition is you might have to take it to another level. I had met old timers, who started out with six years. When I met them, they were on there 20th or 30th something year. Prison is no safe haven for nobody. All that I am going to do my time in peace and go home, might not work out that way.

One time a cell gangster[15] was barking loud to an associate of mines who just happen to have 2 life sentence and 53 years. The next morning, the cell gangster being off point to the fact that the CO's pop all the cell doors in the morning for breakfast

---

[15] A clown talking nonsense behind a locked door.

at the same time. The cell gangster was sleeping—my associate slipped into his cell and put the banger to his neck and woke him up. The cell gangster started begging for his life. He was chastised and spared. See the cell-gangster was a new jack plus he was no gorilla, if he was, he would have been dead. He was giving a pass and taught some valuable lessons:

1. Loose lips can get you killed.

2. Never underestimate the next man.

3. Be aware of your terrain.

4. Know where your opposition at all times.

Living in close quarters with another man can be taxing, frustrating, and at times dangerous depending on the personalities of the cell partners. One time a bully was making it very uncomfortable in the cell for his cellmate, who he thought was a *"bitch ass nigga."* He didn't even allow him to plug up his TV. As time passed the supposedly *"bitch ass nigga"* got fed up and attacked him. It was around 3 o'clock in the morning. I was awakened by blood-curdling screams. After the COs took one to the hole and the other to the infirmary. The prisoner with red hazard material box came to clean up the blood. Next time I saw the bully prisoner, he was humbled and had a permanently scarred face.

The explosion of the East Coast gangs or street nation added another dimension to prison social and political landscape. It made prison officials bring back draconic policies. Whether you in a gang or not, you got labeled based on your look, age, and where you are from. They will log you and your tattoo(s) in their database.

If you are not in a gang it's best if you stay neutral. It serves no purpose for your development or health. I have seen more internal beef and civil strife between the same gangs than with their so-called rivals. This caused them to stab and beat each other to death. It saddens me to see my young brothers in this disheveled state. It's like watching another element of the Willie

Lynch Program.[16]Many gang members do not have anything. The things that supposed to make your bid smoother. At times, some of them do not even have hygiene products. I asked one young brother, who was my homeboy, what was the benefit of being a gang member, especially while doing time? He tried to run some nonsense to me about being in the gang since he was young, the Black Panther Party (BPP), and being a part of a cleaner set. As I talked to him, I saw he had nothing. While he was on the yard cleaning up their gang misinformation, I placed a care-package in his locker and left the book *Survival Pending Revolution* by Paul Alkebulan (An original BPP and college professor). He was another ranking member I had met, who had nothing but was willing to die and already had lost his freedom for his gang.

I have seen supposedly high-ranking members sent lower ranking members on dummy missions. Things they wouldn't do themselves. In the end, a lot of brothers catch a more serious felony than the one that imprisoned them. As well as get shipped to one of the highest security level plantation. They will be there for at least five years.

Witnessing crazy shit on a daily base starts to desensitize you. Your natural instinct to empathize with a person is weakened or destroyed. The people you care about only include those in your crew, religion, way of life, or thinking. Everybody else on some level is the enemy: physically or ideologically.

---

[16] Learn about it.

Family & Friends

"Many times, the decisions we make affect and hurt your closest friends and family the most." Lex Luger

In your fall from grace the true faces—masks fall off—family and friends are revealed. Society overwhelms most people striving to survive making them think less or care less about how you are living in Hades. In other cases, out-of-sight, out-of-mind. How you respond to your dejected state will determine how you will do your time. If you remind people of what you did for them, you just made yourself look weak. Never feel like people owe you because you did a favor for them. Make no mistake it's going to be hard, no matter how you accept it. Some people mentality will break and get on medication. Others will choose death by their own hands. Some will seek comforter in another male's arm. The rest will accept it and grow hardcore: militant or predatory.

Those who think they can maintain a relationship with their woman is in for a big surprise. If she is a stand-up female and you got less than 5 years, it's plausible. But if you have a double-digit bid, hang it up. You are insane if you expect any woman to ride with you. If you really care about her, you would encourage her to go live her life. As well you have the prison system which is designed to discourage relationships. They will harass and humiliate your woman (and your family members) coming to see you. By default dehumanize her (them) in the process. Phone calls will be too much, and you will be shipped far away making travel difficult.

Your family will do what they can, but their lives and daily challenges will take first priority. You should expect this. I have seen many people not handle this well. Your family will never tell you everything going on in the household because they don't want to burden you. And realistically what can you do to improve the situation. Other family members you will not hear from them at all. Some will just write you off. Not everybody can deal with a relative on the inside. ***Don't take it personally***.

As far as friends are concerned. It's the people you least suspect that's going to show you the most love if you weren't a piece of shit. The team you were in the streets with are on their way in or just don't care, prison is part of the lifestyle. You are going to have to realize early the law of reciprocity doesn't exist in everybody's heart or code of conduct. The flipside is how many people did you write that was in prison? Prison at its core is a lonely experience.

If you do not shut down unnecessary emotions and concepts about family and friends, you are not going to make it. You need all your attention to be focused on where you are at. The danger is extremely real. No man can live in two worlds.

In Prison, you will form alliances and build bonds with men. Some of them will have different backgrounds and ideas on life; at times, the point of views will interlock other times conflict. Be extremely careful of who you bring in your circle. A bad judgment can cost you. I have met people who weren't worth a penny, while others were 24 karat solid gold stand-up men. You see what a man is made of when everybody is on the same playing field. Who maintains a high grade of character when nothing is going his way? You will see the test of strength of a man's character as well as yours. You have to learn to read people by watching their moves and how they interact. You can tell who's who in a matter of minutes. Who you choose to walk with will have a direct reflection on you. Lions don't move with hyenas.

Guerrilla Thinking and Urban Refinement

"The whole of science is nothing more than a refinement of everyday thinking." Albert Einstein

The main thing about incarceration is you are going to have to make a choice. Are you going to remain the same and study street philosophy? Are you going to learn a better way to do the same thing or a new hustle from an old fool, whose life consists of touring prisons? Or will you be courageous and transform your pre-incarcerated thinking to be the best you? But if you are not dissatisfied with being a half-dead commodity and living with the quasi-dead, as well as being ruled over by mental midgets, then you probably are a zombie.

The catalyst for transformation for me started when the judge slammed that gravel after my guilty verdict. I thought to myself, this is what I get for following the codes of the street and being a stand-up dude.

FIFTY-FIVE YEARS!

I guess I should have been happy because I was facing life plus 28 years. Reporting this to my father, who already heard, was one of the lowest points in my life. No son should hear that level of hurt transmitted in his father's voice. I didn't even use my whole click.[17]I went to my bunk and wrapped up in a sheet forming a cocoon. Why? For I could cry in peace and go to sleep letting the tears wash another layer of who I thought was me away.

When I awaken I began to question all the ideas and values I was taught in the streets. I would come to learn two powerful key terms and use them like surgical scalpels. They were introspection and retrospection. I realize that I had to emerge myself in a soul-searching mission. This is when my self-discovery truly began. The transformation of the criminal mentality to one of Righteousness.

---

[17] It is a timed phone call.

When I talk about righteousness I am not coming from a religious perspective, but one of self-evaluation, self-mastery, and in tune with Universal Divine Law and Order. The inherent divine compass that exists inside of you.

As I became a big brother to those around me, I understood that I had to reflect a model of manhood other than what was expected from being a convict. Surrendering to your lower reptilian brain is easy. But to be a progressive thinker and practice behavioral refinement and adjustment was a challenge. Why? The prison atmosphere, convict mentality of others, and poor character CO's (and administration(s)); all summon you to surrender to the animal. You have to exercise supreme discipline, or you will become reactionary and a slave to other people's moves. I had to swallow things that offended my false pride. I never mastered it but became a savant of managing it.

When you wake out of your illusionary state of being a *"real nigga"* you become political to what's happening around you. You know from your first day in prison that there is no such thing as rehabilitation. As you develop your knowledge through studying, you understand why. At some point, you will ask yourself, how do I break pass the limited expectation of those who benefit from my situation politically or/and economically?

I will say can't practice complete righteousness in a diabolic atmosphere. One time I was faced with a decision to kill another prisoner. He had done an act of violence to one of my younger brothers and student at that time. I was 29 years old, had been in prison for nine years, and about to turn into a hypocrite in my mother's eye. It was the calmest choice I had ever made. I let one tear for my mother drop. I resolved in my mind that the next move automatically made me eligible for the death penalty. I was already locked up on a murder charge. The only thing that interfered with my plan is that I didn't have a banger. I requested one from the older brothers I rolled with. They gave lip service to my irrational mind. They weighed the situation for themselves, weighed my character, weighed our bonds, and made a decision that saved me from a possibly hot shot in the arm. I am usually rational, but they saw I wasn't because of my bond with the younger brother. They knew I was serious, extremely disciplined, and never talked about my former street life. We only communicated about progressive thoughts and ideas. They understood if they would have given me that banger, I would have killed that prisoner. In the process got death by the state or had gotten natural life in prison. I am still grateful to those brothers (Life and Atl) to this day.

Some may question why I didn't have a banger. The same reason I hung my guns up before I got locked up in 1995. I made a conscious choice not to. When you know you'll get busy and meet aggression with equal or more aggression, and you are striving to change, you have to eliminate certain factors in your life. I was navigating a path out the streets at 20 years old. I knew other options were out there. I didn't like the person I had become. On a very real level the longer you stay in the streets, the more you transform into an animal. Getting comfortable with violence is easy. I knew in my core this wasn't me. It was a fiction I had created by choices I made.

One of the hardest things to do is to alter your thinking from your street persona grata to a progressive urban guerilla thinker. The greatest wars are fought with thoughts and ideas. The first terrain you have to conquer is your own mind. The reason I use guerrilla is my personal nod to intellectual guerillas like Walter Rodney and George Jackson who represented the same concepts but demonstrated in two different arenas. A guerrilla uses every resource available to improve his/her position strategically, knowing they do not have the same resources as opponent(s). I am a thought terrorist to the powers that be.

You can study the concept of guerrilla thinking from those who have the least. This was shown with clarity with the birth of Hip-Hop (until about the mid-nineties) before it was usurped, the gobbling up of urban radio station, the consolidation of major record; and niggerisms and hoe bitches was commoditized. You also see this concept in prison with the ingenuity of prisoners. The way they make things, the channels created to communicate, all done to carve out a little sanity for themselves.

Once you start to think and move differently from the limited expectations of others a few things happen. You become an agent for change; which means you are a model of a man that prison officials do not want to exist. As long as you Joe Coon, Billy the Bad Ass, Religious Ali or Praying Thomas you are acceptable to the status quo. But once you associate yourself with any ideas that take you out the slave-making progress then you a threat to the status quo. You get labeled militant. If you are a Black American, it carries the undertone that you hate Caucasians people, and most people shy away from this. It also conjures up images of the 1960's, especially the utter destruction of Black groups that did not have mainstream views.

Like I stated elsewhere prison is not designed to so-called rehabilitate you. When you break through the chains on your mind, you start to become analytical, using different tools of thinking then the ones you got on the street and/or in their dismal poor school system. You start developing yourself from the curriculum you set. You start to understand the intrinsic values that form the root foundation of this country. So now you are a wild card because prison can only exist with chaos. If you break away from the revolving door syndrome and become Harriet Tubman for others, then you become a disruptive element to them.

Why?

Once understanding saturates in your mind that there is a minimal level of respect men should have nowhere they are at. You walk with no fear, but in the official eyes, your two biggest sins are:

(1) That you challenge their unjust policy and situations.

(2) You teach others how to think and interpret reality for their own benefit.

The flipside of starting to think different and only dealing with radical political ideology will have slipping into the realm of extremism. I have seen this play out with brothers who got caught up in the New Black Panther or New Afrikan Black Panther or Maoism rhetoric. When you combine that with being on the highest security levels of oppression, the battle become less strategic and more physical (which they can't win). They lose sight of the overall goal—getting out of prison or helping others get out and stay out.

Why is it hard to reform the street mind?

The streets provide an addiction that nobody will readily admit. When you know that your respect is real amongst your crew and amongst other crews by force or choice. That woman has sex with you on the strength that your name rings a little or lot. That you live outside of what society dictate is the norm, and you don't fear, or care about the consequences. This makes it harder to refine your thinking. Another set of structure has to be set up in your mind for you to process reality in a different mode of thinking. That's a truth that most liberal-minded white people don't understand. They too busy coming with a Jane Goodall point of view like they going to save monkeys. But the credible messenger knows from experience and have a better measure of the dosage needed to heal an addictive mind.

In the end, there are 3 types of prisoners: men, cowards, and animals. How you conduct yourself from day one will determine who or what you are. And only two types of men exit prison. The broken or unbroken man, that's it!

Understanding Part Two: A more personal look at my journey

"I don't think there's much a person could say about me. My gangster's never been on trial." Beanie Sigel

March 23, 1995 is laser etched in my memory. A rainy lazy Wednesday. I had no intentions of going to my old hood Bushwick or leaving the house. I was in reflection mode. Where was my life really going? I was doing the music thing which was a money pit. I had gone to a meeting with a fella I had fronted cash too. I knew a half a million dollars was on the table. A piece of that I was getting off top. I was also thinking how CUNY had misplaced my paperwork and now I had to start school in the Fall. My dwindling bankroll was gnawing at me. I was weighing my options. I had an offer to go to Virginia and eat with some of my people. But that was a more in-depth commitment. I was not ready to give into it. I knew I would have to carry a gun daily again. A few months ago I celebrated my birthday down there. I had to hold my man down on a money pick up. I knew with the drug game came the gun game. The potential for murder was just in an eye twitch. I was at an impasse in my life trying to figure out my way.

I got a call from a brother I was cool with. He was like you want to smoke. *"I was like yeah, get a Dutch Masters, and get me a 40oz of OE."* The thing was I had stopped drinking 40oz about 6 months ago. I got dressed to go meet him and his people.

As we are out in the drizzly rain doing our thing. I saw 3 people walking. How they were walking, I knew they were plainclothes cops. As they got closer, I could see they were all short. I wonder who had partner these tiny policemen together, two white and one Negro. They didn't ask for no ID they knew we were from around there. The Black one goes into his dog and pony show. I guess he was trying to compensate for his size. We were not disrespectful to them. I had got tired of this cop talking. I waved my hand for him to go and said, *"You dismissed,"* put on my raincoat hoodie and turned my back on him. He didn't like that too much. I was handcuffed and walked to the precinct for a fine.

At the housing precinct, some nice-looking Latina cop was like I see you around. Then started asking me about some dude out there that I only knew by name. I never saw this fella in my life because I didn't hang out there. I told her don't be asking me no *"fucking questions."* I am letting my disdain for the police ooze out. While I was there talking nonsense, Brooklyn Homicide from North Division came in with a warrant for my arrest. The Latina cop was like you have a murder warrant from Virginia (VA). I was like so, I'll be back in 9 months, staying in gangster mode. What I learned is when the jig is up it's up. You must man up for the road to come. This is what most snitches don't want to do. Everybody that breaks the law knows the possible outcome. I tied my Tims up because I knew I had a long hike ahead of me.

I never got that fine.

As the homicide Dees[18] were taking me to their car, my parents were coming to the precinct. They knew immediately the situation I was in was extremely serious. No child should witness his parents in such a dejected and helpless state. That was like a dagger in my heart. That wasn't my first time being arrested, but it was there first time seeing me arrested. That put a temporary crack in my gangster veneer.

My parents got smaller in the window as I was being drove away. My crack got sealed up. It's work call. These Dees were the nicest police I have ever met. Why? Because I didn't have a New York case. They were doing VA a favor. They told me we weren't going to look for me anymore. The only reason they came out to Queens today was because they had nothing else to do. I guess that's why murders don't get solved a lot in Brooklyn. But I already peeped the game they were playing. So, I played right along with them. They got to their objective and asked, *"where do you hang out at?"* I said Bushwick. That's when they got extra sugary.

---

[18] Detectives

They started talking about bodies[19] out there. If I knew anything they could keep me in New York for a year or more. I just smiled, shook head, and said I don't know anything. I don't even know why you got me in handcuffs. They laughed. But in my mind, I was like fuck Sammy the Bull. Cops now think everybody wants to turn into a rat. We kept up our charade the whole ride on the BQE Expressway.

If you have never been arrested, it is a long process. When I was at their headquarters, I took a nap and let the high wear off. I knew at my next stop, I would have to put on another mask. Hours passed before I was finally taken to central booking. Before they released me one of the cops squeeze my arm muscles and was like you can take care of yourself. And I hope everything works out in VA. He had genuine respect for me because he knew I was old school at the ripe old age of 20. He knew I lived by the old codes.

My other mask was on now. Brooklyn's central booking is where the grimiest of the grimiest reside. I am going to the pens fresh with all brand-new gear on surrounded by fiends, bums, and dirty niggas. I already knew the protocol: attack first. I was born in Brooklyn and bred in Bushwick.

It was Wednesday, but the pens were packed like a weekend. The first pen I was in had slave ship standing room. I was thinking how the fuck did all these people get locked up on a Wednesday. It had to be a sweep on a drug strip. I saw a few people with their work uniforms on.

Once I saw the judge I knew I wasn't getting any bail. I didn't have a New York charge. When I was done, I was taken to a less crowded pen. I was able to get a sit on a bench. Now if you have never been inside of the pen let me describe it for you. It can hold like 20 or 30 men. The floor is filthy. Someone is going to be laying on it withdrawing from heroin. The cell had no lights. It felt more like a cave. It's a small area with a toilet. The only thing I knew dudes did in there was go behind the partition and squeeze a razor out their ass. That's called stuffin'.

---

[19] Murders

It was a crew in there smoking a flavor of weed called chocolate. They were eyeing me. I was solo dressed fashionable in Eddie Bauer, Guess, and wearing a fresh pair of Timberland chukkas. I knew what thought was running through their hazy minds. I didn't give a fuck because anything they wanted would have to be taken in blood. I stayed relaxed. They knew from my manner that's what it was. I wasn't willingly giving them shit. That's the code. They were hesitant. I knew they weren't about it. I wasn't prey or predator, but more like a mongoose ready to get it on with cobras.

My next stop was a smaller pen. I was going to be processed to Brooklyn House instead of going to Rikers Island. Now in an interesting turn of events, it was me, a Puerto Rican (PR) cat, and one of the cobras. Life is funny like that advantageous change in a blink of an eye. I wasn't on no bullshit and dude unconsciously surrender by laying on the floor leaving the bench for me and my PR peer.

This PR cat and I hit it off. I don't know why some people are easy to click with. He had a different mentality than me. He loved this jail shit. He offered me one of the razors he had sewn into his jeans. He was jail ready. He had just left Brooklyn House the week prior. He knew he was going back to the six-floor where he was beefing with a few dudes. I was being entertained by his stories. I am like damn, me and this cat the same age, but his whole life revolved around some jail shit. I can tell he was a good brother though, just playing the hand he was dealt.

Next

"Prison is the only form of public housing that the government has truly invested in over the past 5 decades." Marc Lamont Hill

I was going to my next designation I can't remember if it was the fifth or seven-floor. All I knew was that I had a long road ahead of me to freedom. Knowing that you will eventually go to trial for your life is a different experience. It places your mind in a surreal state. I definitely knew I wasn't going to be about jail politics. That consisted of who controlled the phone and TV. If I was going to survive and have the least amount of problems, I had to be visible in the dayroom area.

When I walked into this cellblock, it felt like I was sent back into a time warp to a prison movie. I was being sized up soon as the gates buzzed. A lot of people lose their first battle right there. You can't be nervous or come off like you are a gorilla because either scent will alert the wolves—they definitely have the terrain advantage. I walked through the gate with my bedding and understood I was already under observation. I had to walk down the whole tier because I was in the last cell 15.

The dayroom was smoky and packed. A dude that looked like an action figure walked by me on the way to the shower. You can tell the cats that come in and out of jail. They are extremely muscular, lean and give off a comfortability like they are home. I could never get used to living sub-par.

I went to my cell and paused a moment before I entered it. I thought for a second how tiny it was. It could not have been more than 3 x 6. The bed was on the wall and two pieces of metal sticking out masquerading like a chair and desk. It also had some combo toilet and sink gizmo. This really was 3 walls and a cell door.

I made up my mat because to call it anything else would been an insult. I thought about how a few weeks ago I was on a ski trip. Now I am in the beginning stages of a fight my freedom. It didn't cross my mind that I would blow trial. Even though one of my partners already blew trial and two niggers were snitching. That's the way a real *"G"* prepare for a battle. You never think about losing no matter how much the odds are against you. I guess it's that Nat Turner spirit that resides in alphas.

After being in the cell for 20 minutes, I headed for the Jac.[20] I wanted to use it to let my people know where I was at. It was free, and nobody said nothing when I got on it. An open jac? Prison politics dictate that whoever runs the jac controls the house. I made my call and stepped into the dayroom.

This is a crucial moment that's going to determine how cats look at you. When you are new to a house, you can't move like you are broken by your situation, then you will become chum for the sharks. But if you move like you have been locked up before or fearless, the way people approach you change. That doesn't mean you still won't get challenged.

A person recognized me from Bushwick, but I didn't recognize him. I knew we didn't have beef because he would have attacked me. Why? Because that's what I would have done.

I asked him for a cigarette even though I didn't smoke. I did this for two reasons:

1. To see if he would give it to me. A lot of people are petty about their smokes. I was gauging if we were going to be in an alliance. The thing most people who have never been locked up don't understand is that you spend a lot of time around the same people every day. So, you have to try to uncover a person's character quick.

2. To give off a casual vibe to the rest of the day room like this is not new to me.

As I smoked the cigarette, I was listening to this cat give me the rundown on the house. He said don't get comfortable here because they will ship you to the Island[21] after a month. That was information I needed to know. Then he said, *"some of these*

---

[20] . The jac is a phone.
[21] Rikers Island

niggaz is shook to go, so they be trying to stay here as workers." Another interesting fact that most people on the outside don't know is that prisoners do all the work to help facilitate their process of entrapment. Just like slavery.

This brother and I would go on to have a one-week alliance. He turned out to be a good dude. You meet a lot of stand-up dudes in jail, actually stronger in character than the ones you meet in society.

The first visit I got was from my mother and father. The visiting room experience is humbling and humiliating. You know the Correctional Officers (CO) made it uncomfortable for your family from their demeanor. Your first thought is to go attack them. I will get this feeling a few more times throughout my incarceration. I can see it in their eyes the level of concern, especially my father a former mover of the Chicago street life and no strangers to NY. They knew what I faced because they were in the same situation with my brother in 1991-92. He was victorious in his murder case. He would later get rearrested with 60 g's of MTA money.

My brother and I were putting our parents through unnecessary pain. He loved the street life. I on the other hand was a hybrid. I never enjoyed the streets. I just knew how to navigate in them and did what is necessary. I had no problem going to school and taking advantage of other opportunities. Plus, I learned at a young age that people make allowance for you if you are a *"better than average student"* from what is considered a bad neighborhood. My parents were no different they could see the potential in me. So early on I became the master of wearing different masks.

I enjoyed my visit and had the mask of a good son on. My parents knew the deal with my case. Their support was unquestionable. They knew I was going to fight so we talked about money. The last few months I was doing music, and that shit was a sinkhole. The money I could have had available wasn't. All I had to my name was 2 g's and a little red jeep. I needed at least 25 g's to fight a murder charge. I changed the topic and enjoyed the moment. I knew I was in a dilemma, but that's the nature of life. I watched enough nature programs to know that gazelles have escaped from crocodile jaws.

That would be my only visit from them at Brooklyn House. Visits are emotionally and mentally draining, so upon entering the cellblock, I headed straight to my cell to reflect and doze off.

It was an old fool who kept the recidivism rate high. He wasn't feeling my style. Maybe because I gave off an aura of something he could never be; a respected man. You would be surprised how many people hate you because of your savoir-faire. That is the major reason I had a fugitive warrant. He made a big showing of going out his way and giving people extra food. He was a server because we didn't go to the chow hall. I notice he made sure his ass kissers and brand of bottom feeders got seconds.

I found his behavior amusing and knew people who would have taken offense to it. Then he would have had another set of problems. He was a slave. I knew he was not worth my time. What do I look like squabbling over some jail food? I already knew I was out my element if this was considered the high-life. I silently vow never to embrace this jail shit as normal.

Nothing eventful happened until that Friday. They did a random shakedown that morning, but the true attention of it was to ship a few people off to the Island. A white dude was making noise, and since our cells were adjacent to each other, they thought it was me. One thing I never do is act like a caged animal. They popped my cell and told me to pack up, which I gladly did I was ready to leave this place. As I walked passed the white dude cell, he had a look on his face like I am sorry, but I am glad it's you and not me. He and I knew he would have been food for the wolves.

Frauds like him who pretend in their hood like they on some gangsta shit, come to jail and turn cotton candy soft. I personally knew a few dudes who had reps in the streets and came to the jail and became a Maytag.[22]You don't have to be a gorilla, but you shouldn't be a tulip either. I would see his personality type again just in a different skin.

Who did I see up front waiting to go to the Island, my man from Bushwick. We both had the expressions like I am ready to get away from these Popsicle niggaz. Seeing him confirm my suspicions that we were fingered to leave. I was definitely ok with that. I was comfortable going back to the Island; it's like going to the major league. A lot of reps got made or broke there, for me it was just another obstacle on my journey to freedom.

One thing I would take away from Brooklyn House is an aversion to being around weak cats with gorilla masks on. They are the worst. They are usually the reason behind a person catching another charge while in prison.

The Island

Being shackled and handcuffed on a painted cheese bus to another person, silently actives dormant genetic memories of enslavement. I used this time to reflect on my real fight in Virginia. I knew absolutely nothing about their legal system. I was at another disadvantage. My major problem was I only had 2 g's to my name. I thought about all the money I wasted trying to be in the Hip-Hop game. This was before *ProTools* and beat apps. I spend hundreds alone on weed, liquor, and food weekly. My motto was when I eat, smoke, and drink so do you if you are with me. The funny thing is that a lot of those dudes didn't offer one ounce of support to me when the flipside of life hit. This would be their chance to practice reciprocity; shamefully they failed miserably. It would be my first lesson of many on people's character. I understood that you learn a person's nature through events.

---

22 . A person who washes another person's underwear in jail. It is an ultimate form of disrespect.

The Island is an experience that is designed to make you heartless. It starts with the initial stripped-down process. I was naked practically shoulder to shoulder with another man. A CO was running my property through a metal detector. Another one was saying, *"Open your mouth and run your fingers through it."* He kept barking orders, *"Lift your arms, pick-up your nut sac, then turn around to lift up your feet."* But the most humiliating thing is when he told me to bend over and crack my ass cheeks open. At this point, it's hard not to feel like a slave on an auction block. The ancestral drums get louder. I knew I couldn't be me and mentally survive in here. A layer of humanity was stripped away.

I was sent to a holding cell to wait to be classified. This process determined if I was going to a cellhouse or a mod[23]. It was long. It was late evening when I hit my destination. I wanted to rest but I knew all eyes were on me. I had to stay vigil.

I saw people in the dayroom watching a movie. I observed 3 jacs with only two in use. I placed my property down then went to the open one to update my family on my where about. A fella magically appeared talking about that's *"his"* jac and that I needed permission to use it. I didn't doubt he ran it. But I just got in there and had 3 options:

1. Ask permission, which was definitely not going to happen.

2. Smash him in the head with the jac.

1. 3 Hang the jac up and walk off.

I choose the third option because the first two had immediate and long-term consequences. The first one would have made me appear weak. I would have to answer for it later with some type of violence. The second one would have made me enemies instantly. I didn't know the lay of the land and who was with who. I definitely would have taken a serious loss and probably could have gotten killed. The third choice was the wisest.

After a few seconds of low intense eye warfare, I hung the jac up, but I could see the respect in his eyes. He was an older cat

---

[23] Dormitory

to me. He was in his late twenties or early thirties. The funny thing is that this brother turned out to be a good dude, and so did his right-hand man who had like 50 soaps stacked on his locker. You can tell the people who bid a lot. They are too comfortable at this stage which should be devoted to fighting your charges.

I saw a Spanish cat with a clipboard and an organized phone list. I thought that was the community jac. I investigated it. He said after his brothers got on, meaning Spanish dudes. It was some racial or gang shit going on. I grew up in Bushwick where Black and Spanish dudes ran together and ate off the same plate. This was new to me. To make a long story short, it was three phones: one Muslim, one neutral, and one Spanish; and all of them were either Latin Kings or Netas.

An older Muslim brother gave me his time slot. I didn't use the whole slot, and he asked me why. I told him I used what I needed and walked off. This set the tone of I do what I say, and that's it. It still surprises me how people still undervalued that concept. I went in the day room where they were watching *The Mack*. That was the first time I saw that movie. I got a cigarette from some cat and started learning my surrounding. I knew this was a different game here or the same game but just a different level of it. It wasn't like when I came through the 4 building[24] as a teen. It was only men here. It was only one law; respect.

As my time progressed, I would learn the jail politics of this house. The Black people and Muslim factions had it on smash.[25] When the Muslims made community salat, it was dead silence. The Netas[26] wanted to exercise the same right in a group pray. I deducted that has not always been their practice. They kept asking for respect during their ritual. I knew it was a matter of time before it jumped off.

What I had found interesting was how segregated the mod was. Blacks on one side and Spanish on the other side. For the

---

[24] C-74 the adolescent building on Rikers Island.
[25] Control of the house.
[26] They are a Spanish gang.

most part until different players from the Spanish side start to come in it was a tentative peace. I witness this soft buttercup coward turned Neta then cut all his hair off to appear tough. I could sense the tension rising. I couldn't tell you for what because nobody was getting extorted. Plus, I wasn't part of any group. I was what you called neutral.

I wasn't really neutral. I rhymed and past time with my peer group, who happen to be Muslim. I played casino with another Muslim brother who was 18 years my senior. He used to share some wild street tales with me. He still had a piece of bullet in his face. He used to always ask me to convert to Islam. Then sarcastically he would say you think you are God, at that time I wasn't. My response was once I beat my case. I am going back to make music, drink, smoke weed, and deal with different women. And to top it off I would tell him you were born Muslim and looked how that worked out for you. I could read through his silence like damn I be telling this little muthafucka too much.

I walked into the mod coming back from the law library and it was dead silence. That is never a good thing in this environment. This was the time of the day when dudes would be in their evening wear just relaxing or preparing to go to sleep. Now they are sitting on the edge of their bunks, tense, waiting for a signal for war, or the stalemate to be over.

I went to my bunk. The older Muslim told me what was about to go down. When it jumps off, you are automatically perceived down with who you associate. Nobody has time to sort out whether you're an ally or neutral. That's an understanding you have to learn quick. A slow learner has a good chance of being severely hurt or killed. There are no sidelines everybody is in the game.

I was indifferent to the whole situation. I was curious to see who was going to make the first move. About 10-15 minutes later the leader of the Netas asked to speak with one of the Muslims of influence. He happened to be the brother who gave me his phone time when I first came into the mod. I don't know what was said. All I knew was the beef was dead. I don't know if the Netas had bangers[27]. I knew the Muslims and their neutral allies had a lot of them. I was thinking where did they get them from and stash them at? The good thing was no blood was spilled that day.

The next day I figured what the beef was over. The Netas wanted the same right and courtesy the Muslims had during prayer. I was thinking this is what blood was going to be spilled for. A perceived respect or disrespect and that's enough to kill for. I realized the bar is set real low in jail.

As my time progressed in the mod, I would learn it was a lot of good brothers in there. The older dudes would share insight with the younger ones. A few would express remorse over what they did. Some just got caught up. I listened to some of the most thorough dudes show great levels of humanity. Society only saw the killer, drug dealer or robber.

I would realize how tight that mod was. It became a community. A Correction Officer (CO) was in the mod. It's always supposed to be one-floor officer. One night after lights out a CO didn't want to hear any noise. He attempted to push his weight. He was the lame type that felt his position meant something. Like he was a boss or G. It didn't!

He wanted to take a young Muslim brother to the hole for talking. Now this brother was on trial looking at 25 years to life, which is a stressful situation. He just wasn't trying to think about that. He just trying to steal moments of peace and normalcy.

This CO who looked like he was straight out of a Jodeci casting called told him to pack up. The whole mod stood up, and then the young Muslim said, *"If I go to the hole my people are going with me."*

The CO had a choice to make. He could have called more of his cronies and amped the violence level up. Then he would have to mix it up and get his R & B type S-Curl missed up. He half smirked and said, *"This mod too strong they going to break this up."* He realized his power was illusionary. He wasn't willing to get hurt for it.

---

[27] Homemade knives

He forgot that the only thing that greased the wheel of jail is compromise. If incarcerated men don't compromise, there is no orderly operation. Sadly, I would witness CO's learn this lesson a few more times on my descent through the layers of hell.

The next morning the administration packed our mod up and reclassified us through intake. This destroyed the first capture community I was involved with but not the last.

Most people do not realize that you learn a lot about a person being around them for 24 hours a day. You see their strengths, weaknesses, heart, character, and they see yours. Some of my strongest brothers I would meet in the pressure cooker.

Intake

"Prison make you a better judge of character.
You pick up on people much faster." Suge Knight

I was sent to a mod on the same floor. It was 3 Lower. Now you would think a mod no more than 10 or 15 yards away would have the same atmosphere. Many foolish people who thought like that left a few ounces short of blood. Each mod or cell block has a different protocol. It always starts with the jacs—who control the jacs?

I found out the jac situation was a little different: One phone for the Muslims, one for the Neutrals that was truly open. The last one was for the Netas and Latin Kings to share. This let me know two things from a strategic standpoint. It told me that this mod had none of those super aggressive dudes who identity was based off if they controlled the house. As well as the Spanish gangs were weak in this house at that time. This house didn't have the tension the other one had between the Blacks and Spanish.

That would change.

As time progress the Spanish Latin King faction would grow. It was two Spanish men that sleep on each side of me—cool brothers. I was in good shape with money, so I use to look out for them with food and smokes. Even though, I didn't smoke I kept cigarettes. They act as currency in here.

The one that slept to my left had little of anything. I saw all he had was the clothes on his back and nobody from the streets brought him a package. I gave him an outfit to wear. Then one day he was packing his stuff up. I asked him where he was going? He had the saddest look on his face and said, *"They told me to move over there."* I said who? He pointed to the Latin Kings. I said fuck them you don't have to go over there. What he said next was barely audible. He said, *"I am King."* I was flabbergasted by that. This man was in the mod for a few weeks and didn't have shit.

But once I showed him a level of humanity that they didn't show to him; they pulled rank on him.

I acknowledged who the ringleader of the changing tide in the mod. He was a typical in and out jail cat. I knew eventually we would bump heads. What really got to me is this Black vs Spanish atmosphere that was being created. I grew up in Bushwick, and some of my strongest peoples were of Hispanic descent. One of my best friends who I have known since we were eight years old is Honduran. I can see what the lack of self-knowledge and the transporting of the colonial mind state around did—it creates division.

My time in NYC was getting short because I was waiting to be extradited to Virginia (VA). But the mod was taking a drastic change. I used to play casino with this cool dude about 26 yrs old. He was big 6' 2" and solid like a 260-pound NFL linebacker. He was a Lost Boyz member a crew from Queens. He was the *"getting money"* type. He was the first person I knew that got locked up for having a tagged whip[28]; it was an Infinite J 30. He used to call me Shorty Red—I don't know why. He had already done an UpNorth[29] bid, so he was a vet at this stage. We used to hear the Black dudes walking by mumbling about *"these Germans*[30].*"* He had asked me do you see what was going on? He was schooling me like a big brother would a little one. Even though I thought the situation was bullshit, in a lot of people minds, it wasn't. Jail was always about the illusion of power and who controlled it.

What was going on was that the Latin Kings numbers had increased. They were making power plays. It started with the TV. During primetime which is considered around 4 pm-10pm, they would have it on Telemundo. The problem was it was already a usual time slot for that station at 6 pm. It was of no concern to me because I wasn't watching TV. I was very aware of what that signified. You felt the dynamics shift and soon it was going to be

_____

[28] Whip is a car.
[29] A street term referring to NYSDOC.
[30] A disrespectful term used to describe Puerto Ricans.

a confrontation. Especially since you didn't have one or two Neutrals who was on that gorilla just catching wreck just because of time.

I never suspected I was going to be the catalyst for the renegotiation of the mod's order. It started when I came back from court. VA was coming to get me the next day. I wanted to let my peoples know I was leaving just in case they wanted to be in the courtroom. I went to the customary jac for the Neutrals. I told the Spanish dude that was using it I got next. He looked at me like I was crazy and said in heavily Spanish accented in broken English, *"King jac."* I looked at this muthafucka like he was crazy and said I got next on that jac. Soon as he was done I snatched that shit and made my call. One thing about me is I don't live by the code of the lamb. I saw him run right over to the dude that had brought the negative energy in here.

I used the jac and went back to my bunk and thought nothing of it. Then the dude who is trying to change the protocol of the mod got up and said, *"If anybody got a problem with the Kings can see us on the yard tomorrow."* Now I could have left it alone because I was getting extradited tomorrow. But I knew he was referring to me. And the tiny gangster that lived in me couldn't let it slide. I jumped on my bunk and said, *"Yeah I got a problem and I ain't going to no yard."* Strategically they had the advantage of having all the Latin Kings in the whole building on the yard. Only a fool would have accepted that. At this point, I don't know how this going to end. A lot of my people including my brother came through the Island in the era from 1989-1992 and were UpNorth. I had no people on the Island to go to for support in 1995. If I did, they couldn't back my hand at this moment.

The troublemaker said let's take it in the dayroom. I was like whatever and jumped down from my bunk. I was standing on it like a stage. My adopted big brother came over to me and said, *"Shorty Red I'm with you."* At this moment that was his acknowledgment that he recognized the heart I had as a man. He was linking with me in blood. Technically we were strangers who only played casino together. Now he stepped into a potential war situation when he didn't have too. The Universal principle of *"Real Recognize Real"* was at play here.

As my adoptive brother and I walked to the dayroom, all the dissatisfied came with us. I became the de-facto leader of the disgruntled. The Kings were in there first. So, the troublemaker was talking this big man talked. I let him know I am with whatever. Which was we could fight hand to hand or use razors. He was on his high horse and didn't realize the disgruntle was united and outnumbered them. When it jumped off, it's going be a brawl, not a one-on-one. The older Latin King who was laidback but outranked by the loudmouth went right into diplomatic mode. Which he had the right because he and I talked every morning in the dayroom when everybody was still sleeping. I would be working out and he would be watching the news. We had formed a bond of respect early in the mornings.

I let it be known I followed the rules that existed before I came in this mod. Their position was that it was more Latin Kings now and they needed their own jac. Once I have seen this was not going to go into busy mode, I said my piece. I stated I am leaving tomorrow you other dudes have to be here so speak yours. I walked away and let them decide what the future protocols of the mod was going to be moving forward. My fight was in the South.

That situation showed me when you stand up for yourself and don't fold people will follow you even strangers.

Off to the Next

When I got up the next morning, I didn't really know what was waiting for me. I was just anxious to get my journey started, go down to VA, and win my case. I had things to come back to do. I was looking at the whole ordeal like a day's work. That was the average person in the streets thought process. Looking back, I think my whole generation was crazy.

The day started off wild. In the chow hall waiting to be separated into different court pens. It's done by the Borough you are going to. A crash dummy was sent on a mission to cut somebody. The dudes that sent him was laughing after he foolishly ran down an empty aisle to cut someone and he half-hearted did that. Then he tried to run and toss the razor. He took an unnecessary ass whipping from the CO's. I wonder who put that type of fear in his heart for him to do something so stupid. Fellas on the Island are ruthless and use weak cats for entertainment all the time.

The next crazy thing that happened was while we were in the Brooklyn pen waiting to be shackled to go to court. A dude seen his co-defendant walk by. He yelled to the next pen because they had to be separated and said, *"Yo, that kid that just came in your pen snitching on me."* It wasn't even 30 seconds later, and you heard the rhythm of someone getting the life stomped out of them. By the sound and cadences, you knew he didn't stand a chance. It definitely didn't pay to be a snitch on Rikers Island during this era. The thing about it was that I agreed with him getting his ass whipped. Why? You signed an oath to your people if you are living that street life. If you violate it, then the required payment is blood. All you have is your word and integrity. It should never be for sale because you are afraid of discomfort. Don't do crime if you are not willing to accept the flipside of it. Nobody respects a rat, not even the police and District Attorney that use them to make their case.

Once I got to the court building they brought me out to see the judge. Who was there? My Mother and one of my good comrades. He had raided my closet and was wearing my Timberland Jacket and black construction Timberland boots. He was profiling in the stuff I had bought two days before I got locked up. I was going to wear it to my first strip club that he and his man was going to take me to. He was like, *"This stuff looks good on me, and I got your Cool Water too."* I just had to smirk to myself and shake my head.

Now my attention was back on these two Detectives from VA I am being transferred to. They made everything seem like I was a package. At that moment, my ancestral memories started to seep knowledge into my brain of a bygone era. It's hard not to feel like a slave when everybody around you making decisions on your life is white. I am standing there with feet shackles and handcuffs. One thing that I refused to do is drop my head like I was ashamed. I would never let my Mother witness such a defeated weaken image of me. I stood tall like a G happy to see my mom's.

As I left with my new captors through a side door, all I was thinking about was how nice it was outside. I can tell the hustle and bustle of Downtown Brooklyn had these VA detectives shook. I was thinking to myself these the muthafuckas that got me locked up. As we are cruising Downtown some brother walking across the street saw me in the back seat. He knew immediately with two white males in the front that I was detained. He started yelling, *"Yo keep your head up!"* I smiled because only in Brooklyn, my place of birth, would a warrior stand in front of a police car and yell that. And keep yelling it till I was out of sight.

The only good thought I had was I will be back in 9 months to a year. Boy, I was wrong.

We drove to LaGuardia Airport. These slave catchers were making sure I was comfortable as we waited for our flight to VA. They brought me food and a Source magazine. They already understood by instinct it wasn't going to be any small talk.

Once we boarded the plane, they had to check in their weapons and take the cuffs off me. It's against the law to have a prisoner fly with handcuffs on. The reason being if the plane crashes in the water I should have a chance to swim. I thought that was laughable. If the plane crashes by default, I would have beaten my case. You can't prosecute a dead man. When I think of stuff like that, I realized I watched too many *Alfred Hitchcock Mysteries* growing up as a kid.

The day was nice and sky clear that we made the travel time to Hampton Airport in 35 minutes instead of the usual 45. We arrived before the local new crews, who were rushing to the landing gate. One of my captors asked me if I wanted to be on the news. I replied no because I didn't have a haircut. I figured I am already in handcuffs at least I could look good. I knew the case was high profiled and one of my brothers already blew trial to 68 years. I couldn't be looking scruffy and defeated before I had a chance to fight. Plus a few of my honeys would see me. They always have to see me shining. It's all about mystique.

Another Jail

"By failing to prepare, you are preparing to fail."
Benjamin Franklin

I was taking to their version of central booking. I was brought before a magistrate judge, charges were read against me: conspiracy to commit murder, first-degree murder, and malicious wounded (later they would bring me two more indictments for guns). Each charge carried a 25,000-dollar bail. But I would need two properties to secure it since I was from outer state. I had a few people who were acting like they were going to put the 10% needed down and was trying to see if some people they knew would put up the property. Now dealing with hindsight, they weren't doing anything. It was just talked. When people know you knew enough shit to hang them they play you close. If they were going to put up the bail money, they should have gotten me a lawyer when the conditions couldn't be met. They should have paid that 25g's in installments. No lawyer is going to turn down an upfront 7 1/2 grand in cash. Plus, if I would have made bail, I was going rat hunting.

When you get locked up people forget who their friends are. Somewhere down the line, the dude that owed me money that I invested in while doing the music said something negative about my prison predicament. One of my peoples bucks fifty[31] him for his indiscretion. Then my brother came home and one of my partners he never saw started calling him. They were asking him question about that money he owed me. He was shook[32]for his life. I made a few calls and deescalated the situation. It was something small to me. I learned a big lesson. Always deal with contracts because less honorable people forget their words.

---

[31] A razor cut that takes at least 150 stitches to close.
[32] Street term for being scared

I had only 2 g's to my name kept playing in my mind like a nightmare. I was 23 g's short. I still thought I was going to win. I didn't realize the fix was already in.

The Norfolk City Jail looked like something from a bygone era. When I was finally taken to the 7- floor, I didn't know what to expect. I was walked by little cellblocks, and I felt like these people were on display like animals. On top of that, I realized this jail was overcrowded. When I got to my block, I would see by how much.

When I stepped through the cage doors, I knew I was in the *Outer Limits*. I viewed the living conditions quickly. They had 3 four-man cells that were full and about 8 or more people sleeping on the floor. A shower on the other side from where I was standing. Later I would come to find out none of the toilets in the cell worked. Everybody had to use the same one that was behind a curtain in the dayroom area. It was also two jacs on the wall.

I knew I was dealing with a different mentality from an administrative and inmate level because people back home wouldn't stand for these living conditions. What nailed it for me is when they brought our food on carts that a zoo might use to feed animals.

This would be my first time getting to know VA dudes. It was some good men in there. The running theme would be most stand-up dudes would be facing a lot of time. But to see how dudes went about their daily activities under the most pressure was an honor.

I was in one cell block the whole time named 7A. It was a good group of guys in there. Fights was to a minimum, but one stood out. It was an older dude who used to box. He was about 38yrs old slim and look like drugs had gotten the best of him. He fought a 28yr old, who was husky, a loudmouth, and looked like he never missed a sandwich. The fight was over like most things; respect. They squared off, and of course, the older dude was doing his thing. It didn't take rocket science to know what was coming next. The younger one rushed him and slammed him (ground and pound). An OG type broke it up. The older dude must have had a flashback or something because it kept saying, *"Let me go another round coach."*

The fight was over, and the other dude kept his disrespectful ways. I knew it was a manner of time before somebody packed him up. I was already formulating an attack plan. I observed too many holes in his style. He was too comfortable. My main focus was my case. If I blew trial it would be him.

I had a few visits. I could have done without them. They were a waste of time. The jail gave you 15 minutes behind a glass. Soon as you said hello the visit was over. The people leaving look sadder than me. I guess they had a bird eyes view to my destruction because my co-defendant had blown trial a few months ago. They had witnessed the media circus surrounding his case. They anticipate the same fate for me. I never even considered losing. I guess that was the revolutionary Denmark Vesey spirit in me.

VA must have one of the most draconian legal systems which they only apply to Blacks. I had seen a person paperwork where they gave him 3 years for a dime piece of crack. But gave some white dude 9 months for 15 pounds of weed. You could listen to people cases while in the holding pen. They had a speaker in the ceiling. So, you knew who was snitching without seeing black and white (court papers).

I always went last because I was going to trial. I used to hear dudes whine about their time while I was facing life and 28 years. I was so nonchalant about it; it was scary. Nobody really knows how they are going to act when they are faced with what seems like an insurmountable challenge. I guess my way of coping with it was the understanding that I was going to be a free man by the end of the week.

I was already plotting my next moves. I knew I would still do the music. I also came to terms with myself that I was going to take my man up on his offer and get money with him. He already had a dude lined up for at least a 100 g's. I concluded, if I am going to face time like a gangster, I might as will be one full-time.

Life was showing me you can't straddle the fence. I had to be a 100% committed to the streets or I would miss a move. I already had done that and gave the star rat a stage to perform his soprano.

Up until that time I just saw myself as a person willing to get down, get busy, and a criminal opportunist. I had broken the law before, wore a few hats in the streets here and there. But I never seen myself as a full-time player because I always had other interest. I had no problem with education and preparing for a career. The funny thing is it was a lot of people that fit into my mode of thinking. Life is shades of grey.

I was always ready for showtime. The court officers would come and get me, shackle me up, and escort me to the court-room. I looked at the pool of jury, extremely pasty and middle-age. I didn't see one of my peers. I did see my mother, sister, and one of my partners—a stand-up dude. He showed beyond measure I can count on him in a clinch.

The trial itself turned out to be a comedy rooted in shamolo-gy. The Commonwealth Attorney (they version of a DA) paraded witness after witness who didn't know shit. Some of them from the opposite crew didn't know me. I knew they didn't because I never seen them before in my life. But I was supposed to be the leader of the 718 Crew. I was losing interest in this case. I was just ready for it to be over, so I can get back to my life.

Now the two interesting characters were the rat and the fink. The rat had got himself, the fink, my co-defendant that was on the run, and me indicted. My other man who already blew trial was indicted first. The skirt wearer knew that all he had to do was keep his mouth shut. When I saw him walking down the aisle because he was free on bail, I knew he was supposed to be left at Highland Park. The Commonwealth Attorney was sending the message to the jury; see he is still free he is not the dangerous one. See the dangerous one is shackled; that was me.

The rat sung lies like a canary. He held water like a pregnant daughter. It was laughable to me since I knew the real story. When my lawyer asked him if the only reason he was testifying was to get a time cut he said *"yes."* He already had a 25-year cap and would get 13 years suspended leaving him with 12 years; which he only did six. If I had run across him in prison, I would have beat the soul out of his cowardly body.

I was learning justice is some bullshit that they convince old ladies of. This white Commonwealth Attorney saw a way to use a nigger coon to lock up other niggers and make his career, regardless of the rat part in the crime, which was quite large. I was living the macro Black American experience out on a micro level. Since we have been in this country, you had two currents of Black people: one that works with the pale man against his own people for a treat and the other that will rather die than be used as a tool against his friends.

The fink didn't want to testify on me, but he already testified on our other partner. He told me they were making him when we crossed path in the jail. I had him pull up to the bars. He grabbed my hand trembling with his yellow back self. I asked him why he testified on Sha you were his alibi witness. He just dropped his head. At that moment I saw how weak this chump was. I pitied him. He wasn't even a man to me at that moment. My escort turned back around and that was my signal to get my clothes to dress out for court.

The funny thing is that the rat and the fink testimonies conflicted with each other and didn't interlock on no key points. I started doodling on my legal pad because I thought I definitely got this case beaten. My lawyer whispered pay attention. I am thinking like you just didn't hear conflicting stories from the only thing that tied me to these charges.

The conspiracy roped me in. If that was shown to be contradictory, then all the other charges can't stick. I was thinking I am going to get that tagged[33] Acura Legend coupe with my proceeds from the stick up my man had planned. I would go back to packing heat[34] and moving up and down I-95. It's funny how one thing can change your future outlook. I had stopped carrying

---

[33] A car with the VINs numbers changed.
[34] A gun

guns the beginning of that year. I was supposed to go back to college that January and focus on music. I was striving to be legit. But I have seen in an unjust world that the only legit people are the criminals. Now being a part of a law-abiding society was not a thought in mind.

The 3-day comedy show was over. Now I can get back to my life once the foreman read the words not guilty. I stood indifferent to this whole process. I was ready to go. When this fella said *"guilty,"* I felt a Kunte Kente rage swell up in me. I thought to myself what trial were these dumb muthafuckas at. It's impossible for me to have organized this and the main snitches story contradict each other. I knew this shit would have never have happened in NYC.

My Mother, little sister, and main man Black Jesus was devastated. The dead man's Christian family was jumping for joy and praising God, imagine that. If I still had little faith in the judicial system, it was completely gone now.

I stood still like a G, looking like the boss with a curly afro, pork-chop sideburns, tinted glasses, polo dress shirt, pants, and shoes. If I didn't look like the shot-caller who the fuck else did. I didn't blink or make a sound. I became completely stoic. I was the only person in this charade that wasn't broken. I was outplayed by a bunch of suckers.

They also recommend the time they wanted me to serve. It started with 30 years then went down in descending order 10, 7, 5, 3. My lawyer was adding it up he said, *"you got 13 years less than Burrell."* I had said what the fuck are you talking about and tell the judge to run that shit concurrent. It was denied.

When I heard all those numbers, I had to lock my knees. That's the type of time that make people fold and cry in court. Not because they afraid to do the time. They realize life as they knew it was over. I wasn't going to be that guy. When the newspapers write about me, they going to say he did his best John Gotti impersonation, strutted off in handcuffs and shackles with his head high.

I gave my peoples a half-hearted smile like it's going to be alright. How can you be weak in front of people that are being strong for you? I glanced at the celebrating Christians. You would have thought they won the lottery. Where was their Jesus love for me? I thought to myself you have been played you still didn't get justice. I studied the Motion of Discovered Report. I knew which gun killed their loved one. I also knew who hand it was in.

Now back in the holding tank alone I was like fuck it. I will come back down on appeal. I was wrong. The fix was in, and my lawyer was down with it. I would not come to know that until I became legally astute. I was like most people who think their lawyer was on their side. His loyalty is always to his lunch buddy. It's nothing but a game to them, trade this one and I give three sweetheart deals down the line.

I didn't feel the magnitude of what just happened until I spoke to my Pops. He was a strong man who raised me as well as allowed me to make my own mistakes. When I heard him cry for me, that's when it hit me. He said, *"Mann how are you going to do all that time?"* All that bravado shit released in liquid disappointment. I had hurt the man I respected the most for respect that weighed nothing. All I could say was the best was I can. I didn't even use my whole click. I needed it solitude. I went into my cell, wrapped up in a cocoon, and let my tears flow me to sleep. I realized at that moment I had let my family down. I was loyal but to the wrong flag.

I emerged feeling much better. That cry was cleansing. It washed away my connection to the free world for the moment. For me to survive, I had to be fully invested mentally to where I was at not where I wanted to be. I knew my appeal was going to be filed and I would win on that (or so I thought).

A good brother named Duke was waiting for me to emerge from my cocoon. He was reading my mind and said, *"I already took care of that."* I had told him what I was going to do to the clown who thought he was running the block.

He took care of it.

Men will let you push your weight around until they had enough and then show you, you are just a clown with tootsie roll wrapping on.

I had to go back to court for the sentencing phase about a month and a half later. I wrote the judge a letter. He knew legally I should have walked. When it was time for sentencing, he had said something that would echo clearly in my ears for a long time. He said, *"Had you took me [a bench trial] you would not have gotten what you got. But since you took a jury trial and I have to go with the jury recommendation. I know you think this is unfair, but you will still come home a young man."*

He was under the impression I would make parole in 8-10yrs. I thought I had to do 55 years before I went up for parole. I didn't know how Virginia calculate sentencing different from New York. He still was wrong because the **Truth of Sentence law** aka New Law became in effect in 1995. It mandated you do 85% of your time. This law would in practice affect prisoners who still went up for parole. Politics dictate policy.

As I was leaving the court a camera crew was waiting out-side for me. The reporter had the nerve to ask me did I think what I got was fair. I had to pause to look at this worm person in the face. I said no. The arrogantly stated, *"I will be back."* In my mind, it's always show time. My ancestral genetic code would never let these people feel they have defeated me. I understood my position had weakened but I wasn't a broken man. I really thought I would be back. It was my Bushwick state of mind. I came up in the era where *'real niggaz'* don't fold, **EVERY**!

What's Next

The next leg of the journey took me to a reception center called South Hampton. It was a processing centering for teens and adults up to 25 years old. I was examined medically, mentally, and academically.

I knew immediately that they mastered this art of herding people. The Middle Passage, Holocaust, Slavery, and Colonialization gave them a great skill set for this kind of work. As time progressed, they just got better at it. America has to be the best at doing it because according to statistics she has the most people incarcerated. It's like an oxymoron: the home of the free is also the home of the imprisoned.

My time there was only momentary. I was waiting for a bed space to come open on a maximum-security prison. I would learn a lot about trapped human behaviors here. One thing I noticed is how the system (judicial and correctional) cuddle the white males who they assumed are weak.

One young white male killed and cut his step mother's breast off was being handled with kid gloves. A psychiatrist would sit with him for hours. Why did he deserve special treatment, when a quarter of my wing had been convicted of murder? Some of them had double life sentences, but only he was giving preferential treatment. If a non-political person goes to prison, what he observes will inevitably politicize him. He has no choice on that. But he does have a choice on how he develops his understanding after that.

A young brother I was with at the jail was on my wing. We had a good vibe with each other that would last over a decade. We would be on the same camp as older men and his second time back. I would see him leave prison again having accomplished absolutely nothing but being a junkie. Unfortunately, a lot of people get hooked on drugs while in prison.

This young brother had brought me some lessons from the Nation of Gods and Earths (NGE) aka the Five Percenters. I accepted them because my uncle was a Five Percenter and I liked his mannerism, strength, and militancy. The thing is him and my father had similarities just displayed them differently. I also came across people on the street who claimed to be Five Percenters as well. My growing insight of the teachings would reveal to me that they nor my uncle fully lived up to the tenets. Who can be a gangster and a righteous man at the same time? One mentality is going win out. Whichever seed (idea) you water grows. Nevertheless, this minor introduction to these lessons would have a long-term impact on my life.

Curiosity would align me with the strongest culture that would have a global impact on youth and young adults from the 1960s to 2000. After that, a concentrated effort has been pushed to market gang culture, feminine masculinity, homosexuality, and being dumb as a viable lifestyle. It is no way progressive and righteous ideology could keep up with the highly developed marketing skills and resources of media outlets. They have billions at their disposal to push their agenda.

At the time I got the NGE Lessons. I didn't realize it was only the Supreme Mathematics and Alphabets. They were just the keys to unlock the rest of the 120 Lessons. They stuck a chord with me because my personal philosophy was that I was a realist. I didn't believe in no mystery God. Just like I didn't believe in the Easter bunny or Santa Claus. I had seen too much. My studies on the Black Global Experience let me see Western religions as they were giving to Black people as a slave making tools. Any religion that wears a cultural face of someone who enslaved, colonialized, and denigrated your culture should be rejected outright.

That's why I respect the Moorish Science Temple, Nation of Islam, and Nation of Gods and Earths because they came out and responded to the needs of Black people in America unapologetically.

As I studied the tidbits of the Lessons I had, I continue my historical reading on the Black experience. I still was undeveloped in my understanding and wasn't a 100% convinced that being a Five Percenter was my way. I was political and still fantasizing about being a gangster once I won my appeal. I could see me in that tagged red Acura Legend with the gold trim.

Now being stuck in a 2-man cell with a stranger waiting to be processed was a different experience. The only time we were let out was for chow call, shower, phone call, or recreation. That was either the yard or dayroom to watch TV for an hour. A few months prior, I was moving in and out of state driving on highways or flying on planes. I used to stay out late and get up early. I liked being outside. Now I am regulated to one hour on a small patch of land. As you progress in the system, the less and less your liberties become.

The moments you are out of your cell, you meet the prisoners on your wing. Since I was from another state, I doubted I was going to run across people that I knew. But I did run across a lot of wannabe New Yorkers. Their fraudulence fell apart after primary inquiry. One person told me he was from Queensbridge Housing down the block from Amsterdam Ave out in Coney Island. I didn't even bother to correct him. It was obvious to me he listened to too much rap music. Or he was crazy because I use to talk to him daily, however, outside of that lie, he was a good dude. He had a good heart, one time I didn't make commissary, and he came by my cell and slide 20 dollar's worth of snacks under my door. Had he not told that lie I would have rocked with him. But because of that one flaw, I couldn't. I had learned a hard lesson in betrayal—one I would not duplicate again.

A stranger and I were in the cell for almost 20 hours. I was alright in learning the art of compromise. It allowed things to run smooth. Only a fool would bump heads with his cell-partner and then think he is going to rest sound. Space is limited, and respect is the only currency that exists in the cell. I could never close my eyes with a person I was beefing with in the same cell. One of us would have to go, or we both would go to the hole.

I was lucky because many of my cell partners were stand up dudes with good character. The other ones were alright, but our dealings were limited for one reason or another. The first one told me the story of how he caught his charge. Before he was done, he was crying because he had killed his best friend while playing with a gun. I knew that had to be a heavy burden to carry. He would be the first man to cry in front of me. He was remorseful. I understood and had no judgment towards him and his liquid sorrow. It was a humbling experience for me. At that moment I realized that I couldn't have a blanket policy on everybody is the enemy. I would have to rid myself of stereo-types I had heard about being in prison and the people there.

I was fed a bunch of stories about doing time and how I should be from the OGs. I knew they had to give me insight from their experiences. I knew I had to blaze my own path. Only thing I knew for sure is that I couldn't fold no matter the obstacles I would face. And for every good dude in prison it's plenty more that's slimy, grimy, crazy, or have a weak character.

I remembered this one kid vividly. He could not have been any more than 18 years old. He had the brightest disposition of anybody I met in prison. He had like 2 or 4 years to do something small. Due to a cold DNA hit, he would get arrested while in prison and charged with capital murder. He had raped and killed the local news reporter from his town. They would execute him 5 years later. You never know who a person truly is. He didn't seem to have that type of personality. I realized everybody in here including myself wore one type of mask or another.

My interaction with people became more diplomatic even when I knew they were lying. One fella was trying to convince me that one of my co-defendants was his co-defendant and he was locked up on the case I was convicted of. I was thinking to myself this cat is interesting. I will bid off him[35]. The whole time we were together I never told him that I had already met his co-defendant and the relationship between mines and me. What would have been the point? You learn quick; a lot of things don't mean shit so enjoy the moment. He wasn't dealing in character assassination only fantasizing about being tied to something bigger than himself. I dismissed him as having a mental illness.

I didn't have many altercations based on the fact of how I conducted myself. The first time I had to throw hands was with a supposed to be killer type from his town. The funny thing was we were cool. He had his homeboys shook of him. The Brooklyn in me wouldn't allow me to fear any man. I had been on Rikers Island as a teenager and a young adult, survived, and held myself down. It was no way I was going to let anybody play me. I never

---

[35] Bid off him- means to use a person for your entertainment.

considered myself Albert Anastasia, but I definitely wasn't Ichabod Crane either.

The killer and his team were getting their ass whopped on the basketball court by a DC and NY guard combination. Everybody on the sideline was joking. When his team got demolished, he came to the sideline. He said, *"I done killed four NY niggaz."* I immediately jumped off the bench and was like I ain't going to be the fifth one. We squared off ole school style. I see why he had a gun game—he couldn't fight. My motto is *"come straight at, you win, lose, or draw."* It didn't last long, but it did set a precedent for me. I don't give a fuck who you are; you are not going to disrespect me. He lost face his mysticism was gone.

I would go on and do time with him on a max as well. He just kept sliding down the pole of respect. He thought he was a gangster until he met real ones. He had no identity. He wanted to be looked at as a grimy hustler type. Why? Who knows! The little respect I had for him went out the window once word got out he started dealing with homosexuals. I figured a weak muthafucker has to fit in where he can get in. The only thing a man has in prison is his word and character. Be who you say you are and do what you say you will do. No compromise!

Being at the receiving centered for almost nine months gave me a lot of time to think, write letters, and read. I still felt like I was the man I was when I left the street. My mail game was still strong with the females, my team was still reaching out to me; even my right-hand man who was on the run. I knew my case was going to get overturned and it was going to raise my street profile back home. All I could see was opportunities (most of them criminal). I was blinded by my own arrogant deception.

Big House

"They will never count me among the broken men."
George Jackson

The morning I was told to pack up was hazy. All I do remember was I'm ready for my next destination. I kept imaging that I was going to get sent to some old dungeon-like prison. The kind in the movies like *Shawshank Redemption*.

I was told around 1-3 am and to be ready around 4 am. The VADOC was going to make sure you have no time to use the phone to plan an escape attempt. But my mind was getting deadly calm. My resolve steeled for the unknown. I understood I would always be at a disadvantage, a guest (a New Yorker), in someone else house (VA). That made me exist in a state of hyper-alertness. It's a state that's not normal but necessary for survival. My one singular goal was to make it out of here the same way I came in: unbroken.

My pride was my main fuel. I didn't know what to expect. The Only thing I knew was I was willing to protect myself at all cost, even if that meant killing somebody in the process. A lot of people think it's hard to come to that conclusion, but it's not. You already feel an aspect of your normal feelings dripping out of your body. You can't think or act like you are a normal person in society. Caged status calls for a new mentality to emerge to survive. The objective is how to find the balance between human and monster. That's the duality of self I struggled with. I am naturally a defensive minded person. If you leave me alone, then we have no problems. But if you play the music, you can't tell me how to dance to it. Am I naturally a violent person? No. Can I become violent? In a New York minute. I realized I would be alright going to the Big House.

The process of preparation for transfer was humiliating. As I think back that's what doing time is one continuous humiliation. After they search and pack your property, you get shackled. Now, this was an experience. Your feet are shackled, a chain is wrapped around your waist, you are handcuffed, then a black box is placed over it. Then the black box is fastened to that chain around your waist. The funny thing is I was still expected to carry my box of property to the waiting transport vehicle.

Once I got rolling, I didn't go straight to my next destination. I was transported to a central hub. When I rolled up, I saw CO's lined-up with shotguns and pistol. It's more for the terror effect to show you we completely dominate and have you under our control. I respected it because I knew they were the enemy. I still carried a high disdain for the police and the CO's were nothing but an extension of them.

When I got off the vehicle, all I saw was vans, buses, and the herding of prisoners. I knew they came from all points of Virginia. This process gave me mental flashbacks of the documentaries I had watched of the herding of Jews into trains during the Holocaust. I knew right then I had to make a choice to either start detaching myself emotionally from society or I wasn't going to make it. I had to invest in the moment completely. I had to emerge myself into the abyss. The only emotion I could truly trust and embraced going forward was disdain.

I took the position early I was a hostage, and the Department of Correction was my enemy. That's how I was going to survive—fighting. I concluded that nobody in the same position as me was my enemy. I would only defend myself against a fellow prisoner if I had no choice.

Once I was transferred like cargo to another set of COs'. They had to switch shackles and handcuffs on me. This was done to make me feel insignificant. I was no more human just a package. I learned things by going through this procedure. I couldn't allow it to affect me negatively. I knew the fuel I mentally took in would determine my performance. I allowed it to gas me up positively. No matter what I would not break.

The one repeated question I was always asked by others when I first came home was, "how did you do so much time and didn't break?" At first, I didn't think that was a valid question. Then I thought was I afraid to answer that because the answer would reveal me honestly. **That I stop being human.** *That none of you people matter or existed to me. That I submerged myself in the prison experience and became stoic. To survive, my emotion had to be locked away as well, and I developed a battlefield thinking.*

I learned quickly I was out my element. The people who plan the locations of prisons strategically place them in the boondocks. The further you get from city you see cows, hay, and open land. This reinforces that we got you and forget about your family or your crew helping you now. You on our terrain. They must have study *The Art of War* as well.

I am a good observer and listener. I always determine a person character quickly. From the CO's mannerism and talk, I pegged them as some uneducated rural folks. This couldn't be good. People that probably never been to the city don't like city slickers and think Walmart is Downtown Manhattan. I am city as they come with a prominent New York accent.

Intuitively I knew lesser men in a position of authority would be chaotic. Over time, I would understand they were mental midgets. I would periodically be offended that I allowed myself to be held bondage by this caliber of humans.

We arrived at the prison through the back entrance, just like we would have in slavery and segregation. Once you a prisoner no matter your race you become a nigger on a plantation. The reference was accurate. The same politics I had read about in slavery on a plantation I would see come to pass in prison. The plantation I arrived at was called Nottoway Correctional Center.

Before I was handed off like a football, the CO told us all the plantation we were going to. When he got to me, he said you are going to a good spot. A good spot! That validated for me some of these CO's were crazy. What determines a prison to be a *"good spot?"*

While pulling into the gates of this *"good spot,"* I became calmer. Unlike most people who get theatrical before a battle, I get calmer and quieter. I knew I was at many disadvantages, but the greatest was being from New York. I truly didn't know what to expect. All I knew was this was the flipside of a choice I made and an action I didn't take.

The funny thing was a CO was checking under the van with a mirror. I thought who wanted to smuggle themselves into prison, break out understandable. The driver had made so many twists and turns to get here you knew it was a confusion tactic. If a person escapes with no resources, it was a futile attempt.

They herded us to property, medical, and then the laundry. I am observing with the keen instinct of an eagle. My goal was to gauge the vibe. Everywhere is different, so I couldn't use NY standards or a Rikers Island barometer. I would have to develop a different measurement because I didn't know these dudes' nuisances or mentality.

We on display as the new jacks who hit the plantation. We were next to the commissary gate, and a house was going to the store. I am watching the watches because I knew I was being sized up. The other fellas I was with was acting like I have seen this shit before—nothing new.

The funny thing is that I would get placed in that same house with the watchers.

What they called modern prisons differ in design than ones from a 100 years ago. Instead of houses, they are called pods, and they hold the same amount of people around a 100. The pods are designed to easily control a section of prisoners if a riot or fight broke out. All the cells have a steel door with a slit in them. They are structured in a manner where the control booth is in an elevated position to view everything. Even the showers.

When I walk in it was brightly lit, so it didn't have a dungeon feeling. It was two tiers and around 5 or 6 metal tables in open space, which was the dayroom. The CO open the door to the cell I was going to. I saw it was double-bunked. I just place my stuff on the floor outside of the cell and asked who lived here. Somebody said he was on the rec yard. But the move showed them I deal with certain rules. One thing is you should never go into a cell until you know the deal with your potential cell partner. His lifestyle can conflict with yours, and that is never a good thing in a small closed environment. It's the subtle things you do that let people form an opinion of you. These opinions can have dire consequence for you or be in your favor.

I remember an incident when a Caucasian didn't know or instinctively understood this and went in the cell with a predator who had a sexual thing for white males. I will make the long story short; I never knew what he called himself. From the moment he didn't defend himself with extreme violence, he ceased to exist as a man. I knew him as Valley Boy a prison punk.

When my tentative cellmate came off the yard, we made proper introductions. He was a standup dude. We would get along until he got transferred. He was on the downhill slope of his time. So, he was going to a medium prison closer to his home.

The second person I would run across in that pod was probably one of the realest people I ever met. An 8-body count killer, who didn't act like one or tried to play tough. He pulled up on me when I was looking out the cell door. He was a cell-house[36] worker and stopped by the door and said, *"I know you."* My antennas went all the way up because my case was high profile. I am thinking I will have to get busy with this cat. He might be peoples with the person who got deceased. I was at a disadvantage because I had no contacts yet to get a banger. I knew however if it went down I was going to defend myself.

Since coming into the pod, I didn't speak to anybody except my cell partner. I would come out of my cell, place my chair on the wall, and read. It's crucial to be visible, even though you're not fucking with anyone. You can't come off like you are scared. This is where you are living. The next day I did what I always do. The brother started to walk towards me. He can see it in my eyes I was thinking some other shit. He burst out laughing and said, *"Naw shawty it ain't like that."* Then he explained he collect all the high-profile murder cases news clips—like baseball cards. I thought to myself he's crazy. And that was the start of our friendship. We solidified it with a joint.

---

[36] A prisoner that works keeping the pod clean.

He was a stand-up dude's stand up dude. Many times, he chose his bond with me over his homeboys. They seem to hate New Yorkers. He told me why he chose to stay loyal to our friendship. He said, *"I was trying to kill half of them on the street. Plus, you real and don't be fronting."* I always have been myself. I considered myself a hybrid. I was comfortable operating in two worlds at the same time. I wasn't lame in the streets, and I wasn't academically weak either. I just did what came naturally to me. That's why I always identify with Tragedy Khadafi song *Intelligent Hoodlum.* I never considered myself a gangster, hoodlum (maybe a little ☺), or a thug.

The times I wasn't on the weight pile[37] I used to walk the yard. This when it was one rec yard. It used to be about 800-1000 people on it. This was where you learned who was with who; crews separated by cities, towns, states, and interests.

I could see how people could click up with others because the danger was real. My first time I witness two city crews about to go to war was because one of the dudes' punks smacked the other punk. So, their *"men"* got their respective crews to back their play. I am watching all this unfold like these niggas are crazy—fighting over booty-hole!

By law I don't deal with people I don't respect or don't know. I saw one brother I was cordial with running behind his city crew. I was surprised because he was supposed to have been his own man. He turned out to be the monkey see monkey do type. He would eventually turn into a homosexual, and amongst the underworld players, his name would be no good. Every scheme he got on board with crumbled. He would eventually get a few people indicted on new charges with his stupidity. It's a banger or two with his name on it.

I stayed in my lane and met people naturally. Being young and reserved by default gave me a lot of respect, from people. I didn't need to be down with no crew. People automatically assumed I was a Five Percenter based on my militant vibe. I hadn't committed myself fully yet to the teachings. The brothers

---

[37] The place where you lift weights.

I would observe claiming the Five Percenter's lifestyle definitely didn't inspire me to make that choice. I saw many of them as Niggaz With Attributes (NWA) or image thieves. After being testified on by people that were new to me. I learned my lesson and moved with caution. If I saw flaws or weakness in a person character, I trained myself not to overlook it like it's a small thing. My current situation showed me it's not.

It had to be close to 200 Five Percenters on that plantation. I would see them everywhere and in different factions. I just observed them and kept it moving. By this time, I used to walk the track with an old head from Bedford Stuyvesant. He was cool, funny, respected, and prison knowledgeable but undisciplined. He had a dope habit which led him to come back and forth to prison. He was alright with that vicious cycle. I always wonder how a man could get comfortable with that. I knew I would never know. I was still fighting my case, but it appeared at that time I wasn't going home until I was from 48-52 years old. I was currently 21. I didn't even process the magnitude of that time. I just concentrated on the moment. I was focus on fighting to all my legal remedies were exhausted. I convinced myself, I was going to win the war and resurface.

Walking with this old head was enjoyable because I had nothing to smile about. He Kept it upbeat like he didn't have a care in the world. One day we were walking, and a punk called him that he knew—he literally knew everybody. He went over there and came back laughing. The first thing he said, *"I know you don't get down like this, but I have to tell you this..."* Then he would go on and relay a message from the punk. Now I am thinking this punk is crazy and why would he think that I am into that—I hated punks. I told him you tell that punk if he even looked at me I am going to break his mutherfucking neck. And I meant that with every breath I had.

The old head being who he is burst out laughing like knowing that was going to be my response. He told him exactly that. I saw how the punk had looked at me like O shit I made a mistake. Indeed, he did. The funny thing was he was one of the watchers during my intake process. We were in the same pod, and his so-called *"husband"* was in there too. Right then I calculated that these punks were dangerous. Their minds don't work like civil people. I would go on to witness a lot of drama they would start trying to be pseudo-women.

But I couldn't understand the life of me why he thought that would be alright to insinuate that towards me. Maybe because He was with a crew of punks. One thing I learned about punks is most of them act like high school girls and whores. They chose to play charade with the worst characteristic of women.

I would learn by default why this punk thought that was acceptable by observing a few others in my peer group. A few of them that just came through hadn't curtail their sexual appetite and/or they were resource poor. These vampiric psychological parasitical predators preyed off that. The weak cats mortgage their self-respect usually for a bag of weed and some snacks. So, with the punks, it was a numbers game. If not him then the next one. That was when I first fell but as the years progressed being bi-sexual became some type of fad in society so when young fellas were getting locked up some of them was already into that. They didn't have to be convinced they searched for the punks. I knew right then it was a weaker breed of man out there coming into prison.

Adjusting

"Prison is like high school with knives." Raegan Butcher

Now being on these so-called *"good spot"* for around 3 months. I had seen about two big beef go down. The usually regular fights, an escape attempt, but the wildest thing would be a prisoner getting his case back in court after being sentenced to 300 years, then stab another person over a porn magazine. Now granted it was his magazine but he was going back to court for possible freedom. But in his mind, that level of disrespect of someone taking something from him was too much to handle. He damn nearly killed dude on the weight pile. That allowed me to understand you never know what a man value in here.

Nobody really adjusts to prison just learn how to cope. Some use drugs, drinking, homosexual activities, gambling, working out, religion, table tops, studying, or medication. I coped by becoming a book addict, working out, and working on my habeas corpus because my appeal was denied. I was determined to win. I signed up for the law library on the regular. Now I considered myself intelligent enough to read and understand but reading case law for a newbie brings a learning curve with it. And thanks to Bill Clinton and his **1996 Anti-Terrorism bill** took away that curve. It placed a one-year time limitation on filing your Federal Habeas Corpus. This is a prisoner's last chance to challenge their conviction. When you consider most prisoners have low academic skills and need to strengthen them before they can fight their conviction, what Bill Clinton did was give the judicial system and unfair advantage. He buried a lot of people in shallow graves.

I could have came home in 1999 on a speedy trial violation but was time-barred. I was 122 days late. When I challenged that I was time-barred because the prison went on a 3-month locked down due to an escape attempt and I had no access to the law library. The courts didn't give a fuck about that. I just kept getting politicized through harsh experiences.

The escape attempt would really show me how powerless the prisoner population was against a weaponized organized force. It took place during a Friday night program called. Classes were held during that time for the Nation of Islam (NOI), Moorish Science Temple, and Sunni Muslims. I was going to the NOI to get out the pod and watch some of their videos. Five minutes into the class it was a commotion, I thought it was a fire drill. When I stepped out of class I would see the CO on his knees and handcuffed. One of the nurses lying face down on the floor. It was three prisoners holding them. One of them would have a CO uniform on. Word came down later that he knocked out a CO, undressed him, and threw him in the bushes by the building.

It didn't take a rocket scientist to see what was going on. We were trapped in the school area with these brothers. One, I would come to learn had 9 months left on his sentence. It's no way that he should have been involved. I met him ten years later and talking with him allowed me to understand that he dealt with extreme loyalty. I wondered, how was that reciprocated. He was the one that had the CO uniform on. I realized you must balance your loyalty to others with being loyal to yourself. Over time I would develop that into the concept of *never be loyal to anyone or idea if it makes you disloyal to yourself*.

As we stood locked behind a gate while this was jumping off. I knew their plan went sour because the school building was nowhere near anywhere you can escape from. A prisoner came out with a sword, waving it, and was screaming trying to rally support by saying, *"You hate the white man come on."* I guess he did this because that was his interpretation of these Muslims groups. From a strategic standpoint, I knew he was desperate. His plan went haywire, and the best he could hope for was starting a riot.

All I thought about was Attic 1972 riot and the national guard. I wonder if I would be killed, it was a sobering experience.

Once the CO's organized a response, the first thing I noticed was the Major on the roof with a shotgun. It looked like a 20 gauge. I thought homemade swords against a shotgun that this not going to end well for those brothers. Then I witnessed a bunch of outer shape CO's marching down the stripped in unison with PERT team on their dinge t-shirts. I compared them to the Turtles that be in on Rikers Island, and it was none. The Turtles were all six feet and taller, in shaped, and dressed in tactical military-style gear. This PERT team was surely comedy hour.

As they started to secure us in small pairs with zip ties. I saw a lot of people hearts that night. It was a high level of cowardice. I was one of the last to leave. I figured let the scared inmates go first.

When I got back to my pod, it looked like a tornado hit it. I would come to learn when they called lock down the pods went in an uproar. The CO's had to take a team with dogs and go to each pod to secure them. Then they came and got us. I understood that it's always a volcano of energy ready to explode. Therefore, being hyper-alert is a defensive mechanism because it can go down at any time for any reason.

The administration put the whole compound on locked down status like we were in the hole. Which I found interesting because the brothers who tried to escape were carried unconscious to the hole around 6 am the next day. I saw that because my cell faced the school building. We automatically assume they were dead. They weren't, and those brothers were shipped to the newly opened supermax prison called Red Onion. We were left to deal with the fallout on this *"good spot."*

I didn't know what to expect. They claimed we were on indefinite lockdown. I thought how are they going to manage that? I knew that was bullshit because they needed the prison workforce. The administration would create a kitchen and woodshop worker pod close to the kitchen and woodshop factory. But this was not right away, so the lazy CO's and support staff had to make all three meals and serve it to us.

What really showed me their mentality was how they did us on fresh whites (underwear and t-shirts) and taking showers. We were not allowed any for the first 3 days. Then that night they came with a unit around 2 am asking us, do we want a shower and fresh whites? Of course, we did. This is where it got interesting. They handcuffed us behind our back before letting us out the cell, then escorted us one at a time to the shower with a Rottweiler trailing us. I thought to myself what is all the theatrics for? Why only come 2 am in the morning when they knew most people were sleep?

That would be the routine. It was all about humiliation and control. The administration was trying to gain back the respect they felt like they lost during the escape attempt. What the administration should already realize is that prisoners don't respect being a slave. We compromise for it can be some type of daily order. But when the gunpowder is lit—boom!

One day I am watching from my cell window the little movement on the strip. I saw the medical staff rush to one of the buildings with a gurney. When they came out someone was in a body bag. Through the inmate grapevine word was a fella got turned down for parole again. It was his 18th time. He decided to parole himself by hanging. I figured he was going to be free one way or another.

I was thinking how they could turn a man down that many times. I knew I had to update my political IQ on Virginia. Once I did, I understood why. Most people think because it's a Commonwealth State that they have barbaric laws and politics. That wasn't the reason because Massachusetts a Commonwealth and it is a liberal state. Virginia was a Southern state, and it appeared the further South you go the harsher the laws get. And fundamentally the South is still fighting the Civil War in their mind. They just using an updated version of Black Codes.

I didn't think about parole I figure I would win my case with my habeas corpus. But to know a man became so disheartened and broken is an indictment of the Virginia correctional system. There was no balance between punishment and mercy. The fact that that man went up 18 times for parole you could reason he had done over 25 years in prison. What lesson was he supposed to learn? He was a sign for the rest of us that read **No Hope**.

As the administration went about their business redesigning policy and structures at this *"good spot"* my routine was the same: read, write, workout and watch a 5-inch TV. Only thing changed was I would get my first Caucasian cell partner DM. Long as he didn't smoke, we were alright. He was a funny fella older than me by 10 years. He taught me how to play poker for coffee creamers. He was the type to buy into all that mumbo jumbo state officials push at you when you in one of their institution: prison, mental, or drug treatment. One day we were talking, and he said he was diagnosed with an addictive personality because he was a former addict. I was like it's crack in the pod right now, do you want some? He gave me every excuse for why he didn't want no crack. He had money on his account. My point was to show him don't believe people bullshit especially when their business is you. He was looking at me like this young cat is schooling me like a sage, he was right. My studies on life and personal experience brought me to the conclusion that you can't trust these so-called authority figures, especially when they are making money off you.

One morning DM leaned over his bunk and saw me reading a Five Percenter Newspaper. The God named Isreal had brought me a stack to read. He would be real instrumental in me making my commitment to emerge myself in the Five Percenter lifestyle. He was the first God that asked about me to my man Dog in the pod. He had introduced us on the yard, before the escape attempt. I didn't claim the lifestyle yet. I was still investigating the culture. I had the Supreme Mathematics and Alphabets. I was observing those who claimed they lived it. I knew I didn't want to be associated with those NWAs. One of my reason besides their behavior was the fact that I was testified on. I wasn't quick to embrace new people. But Isreal was a different case. We were cordial on the yard. When he got moved to my pod, we became tight. We had a lot in common. We were both from NYC, went to Norfolk State University, and fancied ourselves as use to be stick-up of kids. Our running inside joke was the Bronx and Brooklyn rival.

In one of the Five Percenter Newspaper, it was an article called *Jive Pretenders.* In that article, it expressed my exact sentiments. I realized right then how could you tell the real from the fake if the real was not visible. I made my decision to submerge myself into the teaching and be the example I wanted to see. I went through a process called walking the desert, which is a 3-day liquid fast. After that, I committed myself to the culture of the Nation of Gods and Earths.

Back to my cell partner DM, he said, *"Are those those racist papers?"* I said read them for yourself they are right there in the corner. The biggest misconception is the Five Percenters are racist in their ideologies. I think the fact that some brothers when they come in tune with the Knowledge of Self (KOS) they also become well versed in the Black Global experience and America's social-political reality. This makes them strong in understanding the dynamic between Black and white people. Some Five Percenters may become angry with their new found understanding. No difference than the sentiment when James Baldwin stated, *"To be a Negro [Black-American] in this country and to be relatively **conscious** is to be in a rage almost all the time."* The weakness of the practitioners of white privilege is that they should have a monopoly on the development of Black and Brown people. They put the *"hate white man"* label on a person, group, or organization if it doesn't follow the script of slave development. White people don't like when you use strong language and factual information based on what they have done and continue to do as a people. They try to make it like you shouldn't be informed of their less than stellar behavior.

One morning I woke up and saw that DM had the whole stack of Five Percenter Newspapers on his bunk. He said to me, *"Yaw are not racist."* It was also how I carried it with him. I had shown him nothing but the utmost respect and righteously interacted with him. I learned never to defend a position that is smoke and mirrors. I am an unapologetic Black man reared in the American experience. I am from the current that doesn't bow down and get off the sidewalk.

When we finally came off lockdown, they moved us to a state of modified lock. They tried to march us in double file to the chow hall herded by a mutt. That definitely didn't work. Nottoway was the first prison to have a patrolling K9 unit inside a compound as part of regular shifts. We were no longer slaves but cattle to be steered in groups. I thought to myself these dummies had learned nothing. Commonsense should have told them oppressive conditions breeds violent dissent.

The way chow and rec were called had drastically changed. In the chow hall as your pod was coming in the other one was leaving out. They locked you in the mess hall. After the last man was seated you had 15 minutes to eat. You ate with the same building every day. Prior to that they just pulled for chow. You could stay in the chow hall until it closed, or when the CO said something to you. The rec yard was cut into halve with one building on each side. Always the same two. What they were trying to do was limit our interaction. There was no cause for because it was an escape attempt not a riot. A few more people after that would have their escape attempt plans discovered before they had a chance to act. I always thought it was natural for people to plan escape attempts if they had the means, ability, and opportunity.

Most riots don't jump off based on some elaborated planning but spontaneous situations. Every day in prison the energy is hostile, and violence is always present flowing like magma beneath the surface. When the pressure builds up, it needs to be released. Most times the triggers are the policy, practices, and poor behavior from the CO's. It accumulates into the perfect storm.

Prison Life

"Around my second year in prison, I understood that a sane person cannot remain sane in an insane environment". Mallah-Divine

As a young dude in prison, I still had mannerism and behavior practices I had not worked on yet. One of them was every now and then I gambled. I would play spade for boxes of cigarettes. This day I was down like two boxes. The people we were playing against wanted to quit. I told the fella who I was betting against if you leave the table you can't get paid. I knew I was muscling him, but I didn't give a fuck. He looked at me crazy, but I was dead serious. What I did was put him in a position that violence is a choice or sit back down and gamble. I wasn't a gangster, but I had flashes of the tendencies. When I broke even we quit. The other dude made a mistake that was going to cost him later. Win, lose or draw he was supposed to attack me. People watch everything and look for openings of weakness.

After that I didn't gambled no more. I realized that certain things triggered a behavior I was trying to refine. Being in the mix and doing whatever I have to do came naturally to me. It's easy to be violent and stay in a thug type of mentality. But I was in the early stages of transforming into a righteous person. That's not an easy task in prison: transforming the criminal mentality to a righteous one.

Daily Pod Life

People talk too much and try to fit in, and in prison, if you are affected by that disease, you will put yourself in a dangerous predicament. Especially if you talk that killer talk and not willing to back it up. Watching and studying people is an art. I had the opportunity to talk to this Italian fella who claimed he was kin to the leader of Murder Inc. The mafia hit squad back in the days. I listen to him spin all type of tales about getting busy—he was quite amusing. In prison, people love to bid off you. And I was no different.

Rumors in the pod sparked up that the Italian killer sucked another dude dick. My man Dog put him in the hot seat and I just listened. He started smiling like a sucker and said he did it. His reason was he got into debt with 2 different store box owners. I am shaking my head like I know this muthafucker didn't just say that shit. So, throwing fuel on the fire, I was like I thought you were a killer. He put that stupid look on his face. He told us the whole story of how he became a punk. One of the store box owners was gay, so he traded sexual favors out of fear of getting stabbed. In return, he got both debts wiped clean, access to his new lover's store box and could fuck him as well. We called those types of gays pancake punks. He was telling the story with no shame, from that day on he was a prison bitch.

The funny shit was the Italian punk and me bumped into each 10 years later. We were both back on Nottoway. He was going by a different name. A brother I was talking to was like yeah that's blahzay right there. He about that work on some gorilla shit. He ran across him on a supermax prison. I was looking like this cat look familiar. I am like I know that cat. I called his name. He looked at me like the jig was up. I told the brother I was kicking it with that dude is a punk. Whatever gorilla shit he was on went out the window from there. Prison is a closed society. You may be able to wear a mask momentarily but what every you do catches up with you. It just reconfirmed my thinking on being a thorough dude. A fake one dies and keeps reinventing himself. Everyone is going to face some type of challenge(s) in prison but how you meet them will determine how your road will unfold.

A lot of OG types that younger dudes in their hoods look up to wasn't shit. A lot of them was dope fiends and homosexuals. They gave the worst advice to the young fellas who sucked that bullshit up. Especially if they had a lot of time or was carrying a life sentence. These OGs would give them their version of doing time. I watch dudes not older enough to buy a drink start sniffing dope and fucking with punks. They were taking these washed up players' advice. No encouragement came from them like go to the law library and fight your case. That reaffirmed for me if I had to get older in prison I would be a real model of what a man should be. Every step I was taking down my self-journey was making me more militant.

Since I was an outer towner, a lot of the younger fellas came to confide in me. They would share their vulnerabilities and fears. They wouldn't dare share this same information with their homeboys. One day this 17-year-old kid came over to me and handed me some papers to look at. When I looked at it, immediately I knew what he was thinking. He had a life and 15-year sentence. That piece of paper was a legal document stating that they were dropping the life sentence. The problem was he listen to them silly OGs and got into the homosexual game. He had fucked two punks a day ago when he thought he had all that time. The way the punks was bragging about his work, I figured he never had any pussy before. He had the saddest look on his face. I told him to suck it up what is done is done. Just learn from the experience.

Crazy things happen all the time. But some bad choices come with mental or physical scars. Then other people are plain stupid and never learn. The brother who I had gambled with got tagged as a victim when it came to that. He played it all and was bad at all of it. He reminded me of one of those degenerate gamblers from a mob movie. He got so much in debt one dude was plotting on raping him. On some movie shit like *South Central* the Nation of Islam stepped in and paid his debt. That came with a cost as well. He had to join their ranks. He got his X. We used to bid off him because he would constantly talk that tough nonsense. He wasn't a bad brother just a little foolish. I knew when he went home he would never come back. He stayed in contact with a mutual acquaintance we had. He updated me on him which confirmed my assessment about him.

As a younger person I knew I had to set standards. It always starts with what you don't do or tolerate. It's a misconception that you must be a gorilla in prison. Nah you just have to find your own lane and ride in it. You got to be a man. Men respect men.

The spark that was most instrumental and impactful on me changing my thinking from the criminal mentality was a letter I received. One of my closest friend's little brother wrote it to me from a juvenile prison Upstate NY. He was 14 years old at the time. Reading his letter brought tears to my eyes. I set an example that indirectly made younger youth admire me and follow in my footsteps. I learned I was a model of destruction by default. Right then and there I knew I owed. I would work towards being a community stakeholder. But first I had to let that criminal mind state go and prepare a different mentality for myself. I had the keys in the 120? the Lesson of the Nation of Gods and Earths.

I started to memorize the Lessons and break them down through research. I feed my book addiction. I learned to correct a flaw in myself, which was to stop by-passing words I didn't understand and look them up. I had to reread a lot of books. But reading is nothing if you don't change your pattern of thinking and behavior.

I was glad I was outer town versus being in the NYDOC where I would have known a lot of people. Some of them I am really close to and loyalties I would have had to adhere to. Down in the VADOC, I wouldn't face that obligation. I could really break my thoughts, values, and ideas down. I had to take a hard look at the type of man I wanted to be going forward. It wasn't magic, and I didn't transformation overnight. I made a conscious effort to change. It was moments where I falter. That allowed me to know how far out the abyss I would need to climb.

Still living

"I saw too much shit. I realized I had to fight to keep my humanity sewn into my body." Mallah-Divine

It became a lonely journey for me emotionally. Realizing that doing time is your time to do by yourself is a difficult trial. When I first got locked up the mail flowed. I was feeling like a superstar. I would get 5-10 pieces a week. That would go down to 5-10 pieces a month. Eventually I stop checking for mail. I knew I was fading to people out there. Only those that truly loved me would stay in some type of contact.

I was young at 20yrs old when I got incarcerate so my peer group had to live their lives and go through their own challenges. I would come to understand that later. Out of all the females that stop writing only one wrote and gave me the details of why. She was engaged and pregnant. I respected that courtesy rather than just fade out or let the letter come back with the finger on the envelope. I was around 23 at the time and probably lost like 90 % of all the females I was dealing with. By 26, they all would be gone. I figured if I had 5 years instead of 55 years that a lot of the sisters would have rolled strong. But such is life.

As for the crew I was dealing with on the regular they would be an utter disappointment. I felt they didn't follow the *"G-Code"* of holding a fallen comrade down. I would hold a lot of disdain for them. I realized reciprocity was not in these cats' character. You never really know a person until events revealed their nature. Being a stand-up dude is a choice and vibration most people vibe below. On some level, I felt like a sucker that I missed these character flaws. Especially when I put it on the line for these brothers and would share whatever I had with them. I would learn a valuable lesson and not overlook people flaws in the future. I would become supremely wise with my interaction with men that I would embrace and form a covenant with. I understood I could not be a slave to the rhythm. In life, shit happens, but it's how you respond to it that matter.

The VADOC was doing all type of things to disconnect you from your loved ones as well. The phone was a major example. They came with a policy that you had to get people authorized on your phone list. You send them a consent form. They had to get it notarized and send back to you with their phone bill. I was young and the people I was dealing with was young. Only people who were going to do that was my family. I learned that my family would jump through hoops to stay in contact with me. But this policy made me lose contact with people that I was only in contact with by phone.

I would be depressed and not realize it. An older brother I was dealing with walked by my cell and was like Gun Smoke what are you watching? He was from Harlem and about 50 something years old. That was their word back in the day for Brooklyn. He assumed I was watching TV as he stepped into my cell and saw it was off. The look on his face let me know he was concerned. I was around 23 and still adjusting to my loss of liberty. He asked me when was the last time I used the phone? I shook my head like I didn't know. He was like come here. We went to the phone. He called his lady and told her to call as many people that I wanted to talk to on the three-way. He had recognized I needed interaction with people that was free and familiar. A phone call to a female friend reenergized me. I would also start to appreciate women on a different level. I took for granted that they would always be available to me. I always had met good women. I didn't know what I had until I lost it.

I didn't just come into prison young and adjusted to this unnatural environment. I never adjusted to it. I learned how to survive, while others embraced it like it was their home. I would learn to cope because I realized it was light at the end of my tunnel—even if I had to do 28 years straight (28yrs-32yrs kill the 55 years). This thinking played a huge part on how I carried it in prison. I came in as a stand-up man, and that's how I was leaving. It might sound crazy the thought of doing all that time. But that's the only way you don't compromise your manhood or your personal code of ethics. Every man should have a code to live by and willing to die by if need be.

I had to carry my own burden. In my studies of the Quran, it was many passages I came across that stated, *"Allah does not put a burden on any human more than he can bear."* Since the religious aspect of a mystery God held no weight to me, I understood the only Allah (God) is myself. I had to man up and walk my journey and take the lows and lowers.

Once I accepted the fact of deep loneliness and expected nothing from nobody on the outside world I could fully focus on where I was at. I shut down emotional as a safety measure. I saw the erratic behavior of others who didn't do that. They let the hardship of trying to maintain ties with their woman drive them crazy. When a family member dies, some would become so distraught they would break their electronics up and trash their cell. Other brothers would emotional fall completely apart and start experimenting with hard drugs to escape. Then you had a percentage that would seek comforter in another male's arm. I processed all of this and saw what wouldn't happen to me.

Prison is Beelzebub's Heaven and the Blackman's hell. By default, the stronger you become in prison to deal with your situation the more detach you become emotionally but you won't realize it until you are free.

Coming into my understanding

*"Prison has taught me that there is a part of you that no one can
ever take from you, and that is your heart." Babar Ahmad*

Being young, disciplined, and well-read was like a beacon to
other people who either wanted to cross-swords (debate) or just
vibe in knowledge. I learned to be guarded either way. When you
embrace unconventional teachings and study life from a strong
point of view of the Global Black Experience people will view you
based off their understanding. I could never be swayed. I knew
what I knew through studying backed by my experiences. I
realized a lot of our people were truly scared to have a Black
train of thought rooted in ideas from our own cultural perspective.

A Nation of Islam brother I had met sat with a few of us at a
dayroom table. I and another Five Percenter was reading the
local newspaper. It had an article on how grave stealers found a
jar in one of the tombs in Khemic (Egypt) and it a recipe for beer.
He started on his holy roller shit and conspiracy stuff. We were
like you don't think that they drank beer. He went into some
other bullshit. After that, he was sharing his weak philosophy on
how we made mistakes so now we in prison. He was basically
trying to push that Farrakhan had the answers. I told him I made
no mistake. I fully understand how I got here. I also felt that was
feeble shit when you try to minimize why you in prison as a
mistake, rather than a lifestyle choice, and values you had at that
time.

I started noticing older convicts calling him by a different
name. I asked him rather than take the rumors on face-value. He
said when he first came to prison he was turned out into a
homosexually. That cleared a lot of for me on the ideas he tried
to push about God and behavior standards. He wasn't even a
man nor had the respect of his peer group. And he wasn't man
enough to check them when they still called him by his
homosexually name. The funny thing was a decade later I would

just miss him on another prison. Brothers that knew us both was like he just left and was back on that homosexually shit. I always figured how do you get back from different dudes putting their dick in you. That just validated to me that this prison shit is the *Twilight Zone and the Out Limits*[38] mixed together.

I didn't know my time was nearing the end of this leg of my journey. My co-defendant and ace had got reclassified by the VADOC and ended up on the compound with me. They went from A, B, C custody which was minimal, medium, maximum to level 1 to 6. Now level1 was a minimal, 2 a medium, and 3-6 low max to supermaxim. They went to a federal-style system to try to justify building essentially 4 supermaxim prisons. The highest being Red Onion and Wallen Ridge. In a news interview they asked the Prison Director Ron Angelone at the time why didn't those facilities have education departments. He stated, *"We are sending them [prisoners] there to die."* That reconfirmed to me how could I look at another prisoner as my enemy and this was the thought process of the Director of the VADOC.

I requested my current cellmate to put in for a transfer for my co-defendant and me can be cell partners. He reluctantly agreed to it. He understood good cellmates were had to find especially in your peer group. He was a diehard Christian with a Five Percenter name that some Gods gave him for always being around and listening to builds in the cipher. He had the same name as my uncle (R.I.P). I used to investigate his mind and really see why he was a Christian. It was beneficial to him. He also got respect amongst the Christian prisoners. He was a good student of the *Word* and like a mini preacher. But I knew all that shit was a fraud. It kept him with outside resources and contacts. He had 20 years under the new law meaning he had to do 85% of that sentence. I guessed he didn't want to be alone on his bid. I told him he was embracing slavery. He didn't like it or couldn't defend his position one bit.

The funny thing he would hit the next prison I was on. His whole profile was different. He was wearing a big gold chain

---

[38] Two paranormal shows.

with a Jesus piece and running a store box. The cell-partner I knew was gone. I said where you get that chain from? He like I always had it. I was like you didn't wear it on the other spot. He knew I knew what time it was. He was fresh in the system when I met him on a dangerous plantation, so he played the Christian angle. Now his feet were wet, and we were around more people in our peer group. But I warned him that a lot of these fellas don't play by the same honor code, so be on point.

The Christian would eventually fight a knucklehead who didn't want to pay his debt. He made a bad choice, and during the fight, the Christian bit his ear off. That got him a trip straight to supermaxim. Word was he got all the way lose and became a leader of a Blood faction. Prison either brings the worst or the best out of you.

I needed to get my co-defendant down in the pod with me. I had not seen him in 3 years. The Nation of Islam student-minister had owed me a favor. It was behind a rumor that someone caught his cell partner fucking him. When I went to laundry the next day it was a platoon of Five Percenters waiting for me to question me on this information because I was in the pod with him. The Gods had their own reason because they started to come out and support the NOI class. I told them I knew nothing about that and the subject matter was closed as far as they were concerned. But some lame ass was eavesdropping on our conversation which was taking place in the hallway. It was not a secret meeting, just a fact-finding mission because you lose all your support for being a homo amongst brothers that don't condone it. Just like magic, another rumor went out like I was spreading that shit.

I was going to jump in front of it by addressing the pod. One of my partners named Dog and his crew was like don't do anything until we back into the pod. It was tension in the air between two cities. I figured if somebody stepped out of line they were going to catch wreck. I was cooled with that. Nevertheless, I didn't wait for them. I wanted to address the situation. I went in from of the TV cut it off and brought the

Nation of Islam brother up and said my piece. Other fellas who thought they were tough was like don't cut the TV off and turned it back on. I cut it off again until I finished. I saw one of his homeboys move in position when he felt like it was going to jump off. I saw that Dog and his team was posted up like whatever. One of the Gods I dealt with came out the shower and posted up. The Nation of Islam brother disappeared which I hadn't noticed until the God pointed that out later. I stood firm and said what I had to say to make sure my name was cleared. The main thing you have in prison is your name, and soap opera type males will try to soil it. People will try to start mischief just because they are bored.

I didn't realize how serious turning the TV off was until my older Jeopardy partner pulled me to the side and schooled me. I still didn't give a fuck it was just a TV and a distraction to what I needed to do. I needed the pod's full attention.

Later that week in the Nation of Islam class the coward homo got up and tried to butter me up in front of the other Gods. Like in all his years in prison he never saw anybody do what I did. I figured because they knew better not to turn the TV off. So now almost a year later I am collecting on that favor he owed me. He went to the watch commander officer, pulled some strings, and my co-defendant was moved into my cell.

We had a chance to strengthen our bond. You really see the measure of a man behind the wall. His name was good at the other spot he was on. I knew he was holding his own. When he came, the other Gods started calling us the 3 wise men. Him, Wise Intel, and me did everything together. From walking to the chow hall, working out, programming, and smoking weed. It was refreshing being around men you can wear one mask with. The mask of brotherhood.

He was with me when I found out my father passed away. I was 23years old at the time. I didn't realize the last visit I had would be the last time I would see my Dad. I would be the first to lose a parent out of us. In years to come, he would lose both. I couldn't fathom how he felt. That's another aspect of doing time it's no guarantee they will permit you to go to the funeral services. And if they do you have to pay the cost for the officers to take you. I remember one time they gave a person permission then took it back. They claimed he didn't do enough time on his sentence yet. I knew I was dealing with real devils after that.

My co-defendant and me study the 120? Lesson of the Nation of Gods and Earths and read the Five Percenter Newspaper. We were doing our best to research and break them down. We had a lot of tools at our disposal. He brought books like me. At that time, it seemed like everybody brought books and was studying something. That's why we prison a higher institution of learning. As time progressed prison would become a cesspool of stupidity. I would see the grade of man fall coming to prison in my later years.

One night after 9 months, the CO woke me up around 3 o'clock in the morning and said pack your bags you are transferring. Which caught me off-guard because I had no transfer in. We were on a security level 4 prison. They were breaking up the dynamic duo. We just sat there in silence for a moment. Nothing can replace the feeling you feel when linking up with a person that knew how you was carrying it on the street and lived by the same codes. And being an outer towner that was familiarity that I didn't feel in about 3yrs. I would never get up with him again in prison. As I write this he still doing time.

Off to the next

"Agitation is their strongest weapon." Mallah-Divine

When you transfer it was the same routine and nothing changes. I was shackled to another inmate like a slave and then transported to the central hub to be handed off like a package. At the hub, prisoners see comrades they hadn't seen in years. You would think the energy would be somber, but it wasn't. Prisoners find momentary moments of peace. In the worst conditions, men can find a second to smile.

I was chained to the God Sincere he was on the last camp with me. We picked up two people and was heading to Southampton Correctional Center. I was tired and leaned on the God to take a nap. The two people we picked up was coming from the receiving center. They were fresh to the prison system. One of them knew the God from the county jail. These brothers asked question after question about being Five Percenters. One because he wanted to learn the language to talk slick to women in his small town. The God set him straight. The other one was interested in the culture. I would become his educator and walk him through the process of becoming a Five Percenter. He would become my first student.

Southampton County has a place in Black American's war history. This is where General Nat Turner had his rebellion. It was rumored that some of the high-ranking staff at this plantation had ancestors killed in that freedom movement. I assumed what the temperature was like before I hit.

The intake process is basically the same but with one exception here. They place you in a single cell intake building before letting you go to general population. This would be the first time in years that I would have time to myself for hours. I reflected on a few things. I had hoped that I would be victorious on my federal habeas corpus. I could see my triumphant walk down the block in my hood. A lot of people front like prison works some mystical magic on them. They become holy rollers and act like street respect not real anymore. I understood that to be great anywhere, you must have respect in the hood that you came up in. That will always be your foundation. Call it hubris, but that's how I saw it at 24yrs old.

Being alone for around 15-20 hours a day gives you a lot of time to introspect. I was writing a rhyme about my father when the impact of what I was writing hit me. He was gone, and an emotional tidal wave overcame me. Tears busted out my head. All I could do is let them flow in honor of my father. I knew right then I had let him down. He had high hopes for me. The last time I would see him would be my last time I would ever view his corporeal existence. I had not fathom losing a parent on this journey. As I looked in the dull plastic masquerading as a mirror, I saw myself morph into my father. The magnitude of being in prison overwhelmed me.

What is the main responsibility of a man? *It is to protect his family*. I left my mother and little sister alone to fend for themselves. This would be the first time in my life I would feel like shit, an utter failure, and disappointment. I realized I chose the wrong team to give undying loyalty to. This is when the concept never be loyal to anyone that makes me disloyal to myself crystallized for me. I was supposed to be a pillar for the family. But I was trapped like a zoo lion, hoping to get relief from a corrupt system. In a rhyme, I wrote: *"He enslaved you why would he save you."* That sentiment summed up the real Black experience. We put faith in a system that we knew was adversarial to us.

I went to sleep that night shedding another level of who I thought I was. Prison peel back layers of you like an onion as you are presented with new truths to face. Some of them will cut with scalpel precision. I was learning I can't run from the man I was becoming. All the challenges I was facing was ideological. Who was I really?

On this plantation, the energy was difference. It had a younger demographic and the impact didn't hit most of these dudes that they were under *No Parole*. The sad thing is many of them didn't realize they would never go home. So, the gambling, drinking, smoking weed, playing, and fighting was a little more turned up here than it would be with an older population.

I was classified and moved to another builder. When I stepped into the building I felt a time shift. This cellblock was dreary, painted grey and brown and it was long in a rectangular shape. It had a roll of metal tables going down the length the hall. It was two tiers of cells. It was no mistake that I was in prison from the B & W movie era. I thought Morgan Freeman was going to give me a bedroll.

It was a team of booty bandits here who just got shipped to the supermax. They liked rapping young boys, especially if they were high yellow[39]. These predatory parasites watched too many old prison movies. They thought that was asserting their manhood by taking another's. What I learned about cowards is they move in packs. They never step to a person that's going get busy for his. I despised those type of niggers. Some of them were still in the hole below me in the intake building. I used to hear their conversation. I knew those vampires needed a stake through their hearts. They took pride in breaking babies.

VADOC would throw teenage boys in with seasoned savages. When they should have been isolated and placed in juvenile corrections until they were 21yrs old. They made them a target. They would give them a different color ID for they couldn't buy tobacco products. It acted as beacon for predators.

I went through my paces of getting accustomed to this plantation. I knew I wasn't going to make it here. It was two crews of CO's one that wouldn't bust your balls and the other one that would go out of their way too. I still had not mastered the art of wearing disdain for the police on my sleeve.

It was a brother from NYC and a cellhouse worker that I met. We hit it off well. He used to always slide to my cell and see me reading the Five Percent Newspaper or something. He stated you are serious about your walk. He gave me some history on himself and experience with the culture. He met a lot of NWA (Niggas

---

[39] A very lighted skin Black-American.

with Attributes) that was not really about transformation or progressive thinking. We used to build[40]for hours. He put his back flag on and gave me my first. We were a dynamic duo like Eric B and Rakim. I knew he had found a kindred spirit in me and likewise. He was an outside. I was a fresh of breath air to a drowning man. Until you are an outsider, surrounded by people who hate your NYC guts, you will never know the experience of those who are. The psychological toll of those claiming to be your brothers in a new way of life just to see them side with their homeboys against you. When you see that people are not really about this life, it can leave you jaded. I understood why he was moving live he was until he met me.

We would become the main facilitators of a class of younger Gods and peers. A Dr York follower gave us his class because he was like they respond to you better. So, at 24yrs old I became the de facto elder of my community. I was still developing myself. Now I am a model for others. I was young and still borderline reckless. I still smoked a lot of weed and drunk mash.[41] I even got caught red-handed with wine twice by the same CO. The CO always gave me a break. I made it a point not to come to class high or tipsy. Being forced into this position helped me understand I have a responsibility. I was held accountable for what I knew.

We would have the class jumping. When we instituted a Hip-Hop summit, it gave us a chance to interact with people from all communities. I would share knowledge on a political or historical issue between sets. I usually went first and spit a progressive rap. I knew you had to reach the people where they at. My peer group respected strength. They knew how I carried it. I moved with no ounce of weakness or fear. I also built from a progressive standpoint. It takes heart to stand-up in front of a 100 men and shares concepts that are going to move their mind. I always was surprised on how many people didn't understand the greatness and richness of themselves.

---

[40] Converse and study on 120? Lesson and the Black Global experience.
[41] Prison wine

What I didn't realize was my raising profile to the administration. They also watched our growing movement on the camera. They saw the class grow to a good 20 to 25 people every week and over a 100 when We had events. I would learn a valuable lesson later. That if you can organize people and move them with your words you are a threat.

As time progressed, I realized the measures I had placed on myself emotional was not a theory. It was confirmed when I had my only visit from a woman since the receiving center. That visit was 3 to 4 years prior. When I enter the visiting room, she was happy and sad at the same time. I felt absolutely nothing. From her actions, I could tell she felt a little guilty too because she has not been the friend to me that I was to her. Especially since she contemplated suicide one night and I talked that thought out of her head. It only took me like 3 to 4 hours.

She was explaining how her life was now. She was doing well as a head nurse. I can tell she felt a certain way because I didn't sit next to her but across like you would do at an interview. This girl had a nice body, pretty face, and smile. I didn't touch or kiss her. And we use to have crazy sexual energy. She was making all these promises about coming to see me weekly and picking up her pen game. I am thinking to myself like whatever. I was a realist. I told her if you could write one letter and come once a month I would be good with that. I had no expectation about her capability to live up to her words.

Another reason I doubted she was coming back because she was crying. She told me how the female CO harassed over her outfit. It was fashionable and jealous women can be petty with each other. I asked her what she had on. She said a purple one-piece short set with open toe sandals. She had to change clothes after driving 2 hours to come visit me. Funny thing was how a cheap clothes store was down the road from the prison. I knew immediately this boar shape CO woman was nitpicking. But the damage had already been done. Humiliation!

The VADOC makes coming to see you an unpleasant experience. This is another tactic that is done to disconnect you from family and friends. I knew she was too tender to keep going through that process. Plus, I didn't give a fuck whether she came back or not. I was getting used to not dealing with people from the outside. I had to focus on where I was at not false tales coming from peoples' mouth. As soon as she didn't keep her word, I destroyed every route I had to get in contact with her. I kept a few of her pictures and ripped the rest of them up and flushed them down the toilet. I was a firm believer in my way or the highway. I wasn't tolerating being treated less than I was because of my social status change. You get what you accept from people.

The Administration

Every time I blinked the administration was coming with a new policy or revising the institutional rule handbook on the infractions you can get. Making the prison system hostile. Now, these infractions where like tickets or fines in the streets. The difference is in here it affects your quality of life and your opportunity to make parole. They started to make every little thing a serious matter. They were doing everything in their power to make sure you stay in prison as long as possible.

The VADOC came with a new mail policy. On how many pieces of paper and pictures can be in one envelope. You had to sign a contract stating they can read your mail without your permission. Brothers went in an uproar. I am a thinker. I knew they were reading whoever mail they wanted before this policy. Why wouldn't they? They only made it known to get a response. They push so much little bullshit I thought they were trying to start a riot. The policy served no purpose. But the flipside if you didn't sign the contact only mail you could receive is legal. I knew a few people who didn't sign it. One was a young God. I asked him why he would cut off his only way to communicate with his family. He was from outer state as well. In his mind, he was taking a stand. I shared with him why I thought it was a bad move. He did what he felt he was built for. I respected that even though I didn't agree. He would also take a stand on the grooming policy that would come shortly after. He had long dreads and they wanted all of us to look the same. He would wind up doing the rest of his time in isolation, around 15 years.

The so-called grooming policy was the VADOC next attack. They wanted everybody to look like we were in the military. Your hair had to be no longer than one inch and no hairstyles that showed individuality. They also frame shit as a security issues, and the courts buy it. I knew prisoners weren't going to stand for this one. I anticipated it would get real. I started growing my hair out to be in solidity with the movement that was sure to come. As the day approached I witness dudes cut their dreads or braids off. I said fuck that I am not going sacrifice myself when I didn't wear my hair longer than an inch anyway. I figured it already had been one Jesus.

When the day came, most of the prisoners was incompliance. Except for the young God, the Rastas, and a group of men following the lead of a former associate of mines. They rounded them all up and send them to the hole. We would send them commissary because the administration was not allowing them to order anything trying to break their spirit. One day a CO that always looked the other way stopped me on my way back from taking a bag of commissary to the hole. He was like you didn't even try to hide it. I was like them brothers don't have anything, and he shook his head in agreement. Now this CO would catch me out of pocket a few times, just shake his head, and laugh. I learned not all CO's are trying to bust your balls.

My former associated who lead the group of other dudes to the hole would make me lose respect for him. This brother was carrying it on some gangster shit on every compound we been on. He would extort other prisoners, sell drugs, get into knife matches, and fight the CO's.

So, when he came out the hole with his braids cut off, I asked him why? He told me that the administration waved a carrot in his face. If he lay down his rebellion, they would give him all his good time back. That pushed out the doors in months. I asked him what about the brothers that took a stand with you. He didn't give a fuck that he had used them as tools. He couldn't say anything. He knew what I was implying. When the leader surrenders it sends a dangerous message. He was a man, a gangster, and never preyed on the weak; until that moment he was a standup dude. I knew whatever bond we had, had ending right there. He was the symbol to all that had gone wrong with all the Black rebellions and progressive organizations. SELLOUT ass niggers!

The ironic thing he would be betrayed by his right-hand man five years later and giving a life sentence in the FEDs.

I learned you never know who a person really is until the pressure gets on them or something pleasurable is waved in their face. One thing about the VADOC is that they have mastered that concept of finding the weak link in the people you least suspected.

By this time, I was into my Franz Fanon and George Jackson studies. Fanon readings was a little difficult because you can tell he wasn't writing for the everyday person but more to intellectuals. I had to keep the dictionary on standby and reread a lot of his passages. But George Jackson was imprisoned and writing from that standpoint. He was more relatable to me. I would understand why people were saying I was militant. The mental food you feed yourself starts to be reflected in your mannerism.

I had stopped smoking weed not because I thought it was wrong, but it was a strategic move. The VADOC started during random urine test on the regular. Before that, they only did it if a person overdose. I watched the ole heads who loved heroin keep getting turned down for parole. I knew I was coming up on parole in another few years. My charge was going to make it difficult for me to get it. I had to give myself every advantage. The parole board was hard on dirty urines. You had a better chance of getting caught with a knife and making parole.

I kept drinking wine when I wanted. Every now and then my man would give me a few rum or brandy shots. How he got them—that was his business. He always broke bread with me. Prison has a strong black-market trade. Any money that a prisoner gets its disposable. The first time I saw big faces on money was in prison.

One day I was in my cell reading Franz Fanon. Our building was on lock because some fool passed out in the communal bathroom with his dick in his hand. Some comedic stuff happens in here. The consequence was our building got searched and drug tests were giving. I was good because I had stop puffing months ago. It was one Sergeant who ran with the shift of assholes that reminded me of a lap dog. He overplayed his authority or had an over-inflated ego. I already had dealt with his kind. I had an aversion to this type of Negro.

This Negro called our wing into the hall to give us unnecessary instructions. He was sweating like a pig and hyped up. He was like you can't even use the communal bathroom. I am thinking this clown is bugging. At that point, I should have gone into my cell. But I had to ask him a question of why. Of course, he took it like a challenge. He got hostile and started using profanity. I never raised my voice, cursed, or left from the doorway of my cell. I just told him what I was going to do.

He went crazy in front of everybody. A prisoner challenging me was his thinking. He was power drunk. I was indifferent and calm. He kept talking. I just walked into my cell and started reading Fanon again. I learned weak people think they have authority over you and the slightest thing will make them get out of character.

About 5-10 minutes later he came back with about 6-8 more CO's. I guess this was supposed to intimidate me. Sadly, I wasn't impressed. I think they forget that most brothers in my age range were warriors. Mentally and physically I was more than comfortable to get it on with them. These CO's don't train. That's all the Gods and I did.

They asked me to step outside the cell which I did. All eyes on me now. They were like turn around for they can put handcuffs on me. I was like for what? I didn't break any rule or prison policy. A fellow warrior was in the next cell. He was in the hallway as well. He looked at me like whatever. This brother had a physical build like Larry Johnson, the former basketball player. Plus, we were both from Bushwick (homeboys), so we had another bond outside of being Five Percenters. I am looking at these CO's and sensed the fear in them. I was not intimidated and maybe a little bit too nonchalant for their taste. I was six years in on my bid and already knew I was going to do at least 20. I was calculating could I absorb the outcome from this. I knew the God couldn't. He just got his 40 years back into court and was waiting for a date. What type of man, friend, and A-alike would I be to allow him to sacrifice his freedom for my ego?

I looked at my A-alike one more time. I saw he had moved his position closer to mines. I shook my head to stand down. I thought these CO's were dumb. They didn't realize his move. Their warfare skills and CO training were poor. It would have been like slaughtering lambs. I looked at the bitch ass Sergeant and turned around to be cuff. Sometimes you have to lay down strategically because all fights are not worthy. Even though it would have been personally rewarding to beat his ass. He was so scared he didn't even put the handcuffs on me. The other CO's was relieved.

I knew something was funny. I would watch it unfold. I started to reevaluate why didn't I just be still and observed silence. It was the same reason I dismissed those cops on the day I got arrested. I had a high contempt for cops. But I am in the position of keep losing. I was taking a computer science correspondence course and lost access to the computers. They didn't bring desktops to the hole.

I should have been out the hole in a couple of days, boy I was wrong. I was about to see the railroad game get laid down. My right-hand man had heard I went down for 2 knives. So soon as he could, he got word to me. He also told me he pulled up on the Sergeant. That he was a little hot-headed that day, and I will be alright. Which should have been the case, until I saw what institutional infraction they gave me. It was attempting to start a riot. That was like the third highest charge you can get in prison. Then he came back the next day after talking to another CO that used to look the other way when we did all type of reckless shit on the yard. The CO told him MD is not coming out the hole. He said the administration was watching how strong he was getting on those cameras.

The CO was talking about the cameras in the chapel where we held our class. The numbers went from a class of 8 to a constant 20-30 brothers weekly and a 100 for an event.

I took my position as the facilitator serious. I would come with prepared lessons on a myriad of topics. We turned that chapel into a school. I came into prison when it was a higher institutional of self-learning. One of the Five Percenters concept is **Each One Teach One, and You Teach to The Level of What You Know**. My style of teaching was raw and thought-provoking. I spoke their language. I moved in a style and manner that they readily identified with. I was a respected man inside and outside my community of Five Percenters.

When I had my hearing for the charge, the fix was in. The Sergeant gave his testimony of the event. I questioned him. He stated that he was the only one using profanity and was hostile. He also stated I didn't make an aggressive move. I was still found guilty of the charge. I was penalized with isolation, then segregation, and recommended for an upgrade to a higher security level prison. Now, none of this is what I expected from this simple action. Especially since a few months ago, I had got caught with 57 glass vials of oil, which was contraband and a security breach. The same hearing officer was like I know you are not going to tell me where you got those vials from. Then gave me an informal resolution as the penalty, which means I didn't get penalized.

Now I am getting a hammer slammed on me. I understood what it was. I was a security threat. I had no fear of them, a hardcore demeanor, and people were attracted to the ideas I shared. They could care less that I would carry commissary or gallons of wine to different buildings. All that was acceptable behavior. But the mere thought of not bending a knee to them and teaching brothers non-slave ideas got them in an uproar. I was an unapologetic Blackman.

At the end of the day, I was ready to blow this noodle joint. I was taking a major educational lost. Had this incident not happen I would have had an associate degree in computer science and knew four computer languages. I would have to learn to manage my disdain and disgust for CO's, cops, and Negros on my sleeve. You learn your greatest lesson in losing something. I had repeated the same behavior twice. I would reevaluate and move different. The true agenda was getting home before I turned 52 years old.

I lived like a king in the hole. My A-alikes[42] made sure I had plenty of commissary and reading material. A brother with one-eye that worked back there use to bring it to me. We had good conversation as well. The funny thing was when he had first started coming out to our class we had bumped head on his teachings. He was on some Egyptian knowledge. He was really volatile, he thought of himself as some type of prizefighter. During a class, I dismissed his information as being inaccurate because it was. He jumped up excited like he was going get busy. I leaned my chair back on the hind legs and cross my arms like nigga I don't believe. He saw it was no fear in my eyes. I understood completely one thing, if he would have swung he would have never made it out of there intact. The administration never had a CO in the chapel with us on. They were always short staff on the weekend.

I completely trusted the Gods. We had bonds that was forged in knowledge and hard times. On top of that most of them confided in me. I held a unique position in the cipher at 26 years old. I knew explicitly one-eyed would have not made it out there. You had to be a fool to get violent in a den of wolves. Especially when three-fourths of us was no stranger to heavy levels of violence. I learned as a little kid, gangsters don't do all that

_____

[42] A term that denotes a fellow traveler/member in the Five Percenter teachings.

talking and gesturing. I just disrespected him in the most nonchalant manner. It had the effect I knew it would. He knew through my mannerism that the intimidation game doesn't work on me. He was no fool. He bowed out and stomped off. I could have given the word at any time and he was done. But that wasn't my style.

I realized that a lot of men get emotional behind their ideas and beliefs, especially when you challenge them. We have a concept in the NGE it's called **Show and Prove**. It means whatever you say you better back it up with facts. Men get hot at times, but that doesn't mean we have to go to war behind that. He knew I had a better hand and didn't play it. I understood that violence should be reserved for your enemy and a disagreement don't make a man that. That is why one-eye was transporting books and commissary. He even turned me on to a fictional writer name Eric Van Lustbader.

I went through their process of being labeled a threat and getting my security level upped again. Under their point system, I was a level 6 supermax candidate. They overrode it to a level 4. I found that interesting. My counselor recognized they were railroading me to get me off that compound. She would send me a picture with a frog in a swan's mouth and the frog choking its neck trying not to be eaten. The caption read *Never Give Up*.

I saw their politics towards a thought terrorist. I was in the hole with one prisoner who got caught bagging up an ounce of weed, another got caught with 15 knives in his windowsill, and I was transferred before both. My studies trained me to understand what so-called power really fear. It's the man that can move other people with words. In reality, what did I do? I hurt the mental midget CO pride by not allowing him to lay some tyrannically made up rule. I should have gotten credit for sparing him and his cohorts from an ass whipping (laughing out loud).

I figured I was not like most people. I enjoyed being in the hole once they gave me my tools back. I got hours of studying and working out in. This is when I started to notice that I wasn't getting the volume of mail I use to get. It was on the decline for years, but now it was a trickle. The flipside of being in the hole is your mind starts to play tricks on you. I started to make up scenarios of why people were not writing at me. They were all negative. I never even considered that life was happening as my moments were frozen.

I had gotten a letter from a female that was cool with me. She was telling me about her life or how out of control it was. She had a habit of reminiscing on yesteryears. I was in fire mode that day. I should have learned by now not to write people back went I am. I was brutally honest with no filter. The things I said to her made her never write me again. Her letters were the most introspective and thought-provoking once I got passed her old memories of me.

But that was my pattern since I was around 23 years old. An elder God once told me you shouldn't write people in that tone or drop nuclear bombs on them. That came from the fact that a sister I meet had sent my letters back. He wanted to see what I wrote. I showed him. He looked at me, shook his head, and smiled. He probably thought I was losing my mind. I had sketched pictures of how the HIV virus attacks a cell and make it produce other HIV viruses. I related each drawing to Caucasians and their practices when dealing with non-Caucasian cultures. I think this was around the time he gave me a Western novel to read. I take it he wanted me to rest my mind from on all that serious reading. Studying was the only life preserver I had in a sea of loneliness.

I felt comfortable writing about the things I was reading and relating it to my ancestral memory. I had nothing else to talk about, except the Global Black Experience. I knew no female was going to ride this bid. I was not going to sex talk with her for she can use my energy and give it to someone else. I even told a sister I was dealing with before prison, don't ever send me a sex letter again. I was under no illusion about my situation and the numbers I had to do. I was still in the process of shutting aspects of myself down and didn't need to be distracted by mirages and possibilities that couldn't be. I didn't realize I was killing a facet of myself. I just knew what I needed to do to survive, maintain, and be in the moment. The future really didn't exist, and the past was a shadow.

I saw the craziness brothers went through trying to maintain a relationship with a woman. It was really about controlling the pussy. They didn't want anyone else sampling it. They couldn't fathom her gushing juices on another man. A pimp once told me, *"you don't pimp with your dick you pimp with your mind."* I understood it as if you got a female's mind she going to freely stay.

I was ready to blow this spot where Nat Turner cut off slave owners heads'. I was proud to walk on land that Black warriors had battled for their freedom. They got tired of bending a knee and took matters into their own hands. It's funny how a lot of prisons in the South are built on former plantation. I guess why prisoners called them that. I learned a lot here. I understood words of meaning are feared by people in so-called authority. They knew if thinking minds become logical and awakening, it's no way a few dozen CO's could control platoons of prisoners. They understood by keeping people dumb it allowed them to maintain an advantage.

When it was time for me to go, the prisoners waiting for transfers was like how they are getting you off here first. They wanted to get back to general population. That would only happen on another plantation. By now I was used to shackles during transportation. I went to court dates in NY, VA, and traveled to different prisons. At 26 years own this shit was normal.

Nottoway

"Life is a journey that must be traveled no matter how bad the roads and accommodations." Oliver Goldsmith

I was back at Nottoway. I was alright with that. I figured I knew how the CO's carried it there. Boy, I was wrong. It was a different prison from when I was on it. All the measure they tried to enforce after the escape attempt was fully instituted. I was taken right to the hole to finish my segregation time.

I would not get any information unless I went to rec called. Now going to rec when you in population is totally different when you in the hole. It's the most humiliation process. First, they make you turn around in your cell and back up to the tray slot for they can put the handcuffs on you. Then let you out, pat you down, and shake your cell down. All they would find is a piece of fruit from my breakfast tray that I saved to eat when I came off the yard. It would get thrown away. I thought that was crazy. I wasn't allowed to buy food from the commissary. So that piece of fruit meant a lot to me. The CO's then placed leg shackles on me and a dog lease on the handcuffs which were behind my back. I had to walk maybe 10 yards through rows of dog cages. They were like the ones in a kennel. The just added razor wire on top. Once I was placed in the cage, then they took off the leash, cuffs, and shackles. I had trained myself mentally to be impregnable. My constitution was steel. It is not just the social isolation that breaks some men while they in the hole it's the overall experience.

I loved going out to get fresh air and picking up the plantation news. Immediately I saw one of my allies and homeboys. He was happy to see me because we had a few commonalities from back home one being a woman. He was backed there because he stabbed one of these so-called gorillas. He didn't know nobody in VA. He got caught up in a killed or be killed situation behind some drug transaction while on the streets. He won the other guy lost.

He mainly stuck to himself. All wanted to do was his bid then go to NY to do another bid. Some people think you weak when you are a loner. Others think they are strong or tough because they have a crew. It never ends good for the tough guy. The only good thing that came out of the situation was once the other dude that got stabbed up followed the G-code (he didn't know anything).

As we talked I was interrupted by a brother, who was like, *"where you from?"* I guessed he heard the language I was using. I paused him to finish talking to R. When the CO's took him back to his cell, I went to see what the new fella wanted. I didn't pause him on some disrespectful shit. You only get an hour in the cage and R time was about to be up.

As this brother and I went through the customary fact checking routine, we both concluded that we were official Brooklynites. It was a lot of frauds claiming five borough jackets with weak hearts and poor character. Another current was lames back home and faking tough in the South. I always stayed away from that breed. I didn't play the home team thing, but it was good occasionally to link up with official people. They understood what bred your mentality.

This brother was a Blood General. I was always interested in the spread of the Bloods in NYC. I got extradited to VA in May 1995. It wasn't any Bloods on the street that I noticed. And in North Facility (OBCC) a building on Rikers Island they present was minimal. I had my theory. NYC always had crews from block crews to big crews like the Decepticons, BandaCons, Untouchables, LoLifes, A-Team, Young Guns, Lost Boys, BMW, Bushwick Posse, and even some of the graffiti crews like MSD, U5, and TMR. But why the Bloods?

I started to study the Hip-Hop influence with the Diplomats. They had a similar effect that WuTang had in spreading the ideas that they live. It may have been to counter Wu-Tang's influence of talking about and promoting concepts of the Five Percenter's teaching. I saw a lot of brothers started to study because of them. A lot that came in because of that influence fell off just as fast. I knew what the Bloods was in for especially since they are a street gang in the eyes of policymakers.

I also think a faction within the government had a hand in it. It feels like one of their tactics straight from the COINTELPRO black bag. They definitely got an assist from the music executives who pushed and promoted gang rap. Anything that destroys the minds and image of Black people is welcomed. If you inject NYC with any ideas positive or negative, it spreads because New Yorkers travel, especially up and down the I-95 corridor.

The General and I talked till his time was up. We would establish a good association on the yard for about a year until he had to go to the FEDs. One thing I can say about him he stuck to his principles of what he represented, and he didn't bring nobody home[43]. He wasn't into having a bunch of flunkies like I would see others do in years to come. Plus, he just looked at himself as passing through.

My time in the hole showed me a portion of prisoners' minds are fucked up. The noisemakers got up around dinner chow. Their level of conversation was dismally poor, and it centered on gunning[44]. One brother was telling how he cut holes in his orange skull cap to make a mask. Then he got naked, put on a sheet like a cape, and stood in the cell door with all the lights on for the female CO could see him and started gunning her. I could tell gunning was out of control on this new version of Nottoway. They had a whole pod where they put them in when. This pod did everything last from eating chow to going to the commissary. These prisoners seem prideful to be labeled as sexual deviants. If they caught 3 gunning charges, the administration filed paperwork to the court on them. That made them potential sex offenders.

Most of these prisoners where young, in an abnormal environment, had no access to women because there was no conjugal visit policy. They did what came naturally to them. I rather them

---

[43] Induct somebody to the gang.
[44] When prisoners masturbate off the CO women usually without their permission.

masturbate off a CO minus the abnormal shit then turn into a homosexually.

I continued my routine of getting up to study and workout while the noisemakers were sleep. I noticed they kept a few people back there that was seriously mentally disturbed. I figured mental inmates being sent to prison was another scam cooked up by local politicians and businessmen. It was one brother who was in the adjacent cell that would try to engage me in conversation. One session with him and then watching his behavior I knew he was out of touch with reality. He kept asking me when are they going to let him go home, do I have a cigarette, when are we going to the commissary, and what is on TV? I had to remind him we were in the hole. He would ask me why? I knew the administration knew he was crazy. I had seen him attempted to throw piss on a CO and a prisoner going to the dog cages. They didn't come back and break him up. He never took showers and spent hours on the door having a conversation with himself.

One day I was coming back from the dog cages and a Caucasian I talked to on the other side of me started yelling adamantly *"MD turn on your radio. They knocked down the Twin Towers."* I thought somebody tried to blow them up again like in 1993 with a van. As soon as I got in and put on my Walkman to listen to the news. All I heard was Tower 2 is coming down. All I started to think was I hope none of my people worked there. I knew a lot of people was dead. I observed a clown Negro Muslim hollering and hooping joyfully. Everybody was on the doors now.

I was like what the fuck is all that for. I thought to myself Arabized Islam was fucking these niggers up. I told him it's a high school a few blocks from the Towers. He tried to give me his understanding. I let him know how foolish he sounded. I was like this country been mistreating our people since we been over here. And you telling mean you need another group of people to identify with, their cause and not your own? I said you sound like a slave. He started to mumble some bullshit. I just walked away from the door.

I understood why they would hit the Towers because it was America's economic symbol. Just like the Pentagon represented the military, and the White House was the seat of global oppression masked in free democracy rhetoric.

I just sat down and started writing letters because access to the phone was limited. I was like damn life passing me by. I knew at that moment I had to eradicate that thought completely. I couldn't live in two worlds. I had adjusted my mentality at 25yrs old when all my legal battles were over. But still, I was listening to history unfold.

I knew the newspaper would be at my cell door by time I finished working out and reading. The only section that would be missing was the sports—which I didn't care about. The CO dropped the paper off and said, *"you were supposed to be outta here two weeks ago."* I said I know. He was like why weren't you complaining like others would have. I am thinking to myself why he gave a fuck. Plus, I knew why I was still back here. I was a non-smoker, and by law, they couldn't place me in a cell with a smoker. They also used a color code system. It was supposed to place you in a cell with a compatible cellmate. He saw I wasn't talkative and keep it moving. I always caught him studying me.

The administration kept files on every prisoner. They knew your affiliation. Who you call. Who you get mail from. They record your books and music you buy. What they do best is observe you. They don't fear prisoners trying to live that convict mentality. They fear the ones that don't. They knew what transformation look like in captivity amongst the downtrodden. The hundreds of slave ship mutinies left an imprint on their DNA. In their hearts of hearts, they understood a person like me was no full citizen and partner in the American experiment. They never completely knew what's going to come out of a cocoon of isolation.

Back to the Yard

"A man who stands for nothing will fall for anything." Malcolm X

Now touching the yard on another compound that you been on before you might think that you knew the lay of the land. That train of thinking is a mistake. I still had to observe the rules of going on a new plantation. I already witnessed that people will switch or create a new personality. I started to think prison was one big social experiment in charades.

After my escort dropped me off, I immediately started observing the flow of the pod. It was Ramadan, so they were just serving the Muslims their evening meal. The first brother that identified me was a fella I knew from the Nation of Islam (NOI). He was an extremely good brother. He walked right over to me and handed me a tray and stated we will talk later. He knew I usually participate in Ramadan. Nah the NGE don't observe that custom. But in prison, it's one of the few opportunities to get wholesome meals for a month. It also provided a way to link up with other Five Percenters during program call.

The VADOC was making it hard for Five Percenters to interact. The things we would do that is customary to us like holding ciphers—which is our way of teaching, examining, and sharing information with each other would get broken up. A lot of brothers became Five Percenters by hearing educate men talk about whatever issue of the day or/and historical truth. We had to develop ways to stay in contact on a controlled movement plantation. We had to created underground methods to link up and share information. I would eventually suggest and help create a clandestine newsletter.

I dropped my property off. I knew almost the whole pod. It felt totally different than the first time as a new jack. I spoke with a few people to see who was still here. I saw a few dudes throwing of gang signs. That was a new element I had to gain an understanding of.

It wasn't anything noticeably different about the way the compound was run. They had new CO's and some of them were dickheads. Two were called Dick and Balls. These mental midgets specialized in giving you a hard time when you went to chow call. They would harass you with petty rules like the grooming policy. If you weren't clean shave every time they saw you. They would give you an institutional infraction. On this compound, they had a program called PIP. You would lose commissary, phone, and visiting room privileges all at the same time. So, imagine going anywhere from 2 weeks to 6 months without these privileges.

One of the asshole CO's hit me with a bogus grooming policy charge on the way to the chow hall. I knew he was on some bullshit because I had nothing to shave. He had single me out to push his imaginary authority. At that moment he had crossed into a dangers place and didn't realize it. Normally I wouldn't give a fuck. But I was getting a visit that weekend from my family. My mother had to use her vacation time to make it worth her wild. I couldn't call home because the phone company had a block on it trying to extort me to get my family to switch long distance carriers. I wasn't going to do that. I was comfortable with writing letters.

I was extremely upset with Dick or Balls. I put it in my mind that if I didn't get that PIP off, I was going to fuck him up. I figured it was a fair exchanged for putting my family through an unnecessary ordeal. A brother whispered in my ear that a gay inmate in our pod was strong with the Lieutenant (LT), who could dismiss the charge. I was anti-homo. But I still went and talked to him and told my story. He disappeared out the pod after that. When the LT came to serve me the PIP, I told him what happen just like I was instructed. He dismissed it on the spot. I said to myself, *"that punk strong."*

I had been in the pod with the gay fella the whole time and never spoke to him. I guessed it was the old convict in him that allowed him to help me. He would tell me I could call him by a female name. I said I couldn't do that. He knew I was serious and held on to certain views. He said I could call him T. I never called any male by their female stage name. What gays did was their business, but I wasn't going to be a culprit to it. I did stop being anti-homo. I didn't see them as allies either. Their minds didn't work the same.

The same old routine became the norm again. You spend a lot of time in your cell and who your cell partner was became important. I got one of the young Gods that was with me on the last compound to become my cellmate. He still was in the early stages of learning 120. A solid dude from the Bronx. He was just like me he had no family or friends in Virginia. I made a lot of tight bonds with brothers I walked with. He would be no different.

What I liked about King was he never made excuses. He was diligent in his studies, worked out, and would listen. It was almost like the Jedi training: a Padawan[45]and a Master. But now and then I had to remind him subtlety to stay on point. He was training for the smoker which was the prison sponsored boxing tournament. He was in the last one and defeated his opponent with a series of body blows. He was in a different pod then. I was against it fundamentally because it was some slave shit. You couldn't see your counselor or anybody of rank when you needed to. But they all would be in attendance for the smoker. Only prisoners allowed to go to the event were the fighters and cornerman. Everyone else had to watch on CCTV. Another reason I was against it because it was no access to the gym to train. They just put up a list and people signed up to fight.

One morning King was up training and I pointed these things out to him. That basically you are a slave for their entertainment. We were on lockdown and watching the last smoker on video. I asked him you don't think the warden take these tapes home? Then I said he probably shows it to his friends at his BBQ and laughing like look at what I got these niggers doing. I knew he was drawing it up by the look in his eyes. He didn't even consider that. I was aiding him in becoming a critical thinker. I

---

[45] A Jedi apprentice.

would strategically give him certain books to read and recommend others. My library was strong on the Black experience from a socio-historically paradigm. I considered myself politically a global black nationalist. Why because it goes into my personal philosophy of **not treating nobody better than they treat you**.

He stopped, looked at me, and started to unwrap his hands. A lot was said without words. He knew no respecting conscious person should or would be entertainment for his oppressors. We were true and living Gods, so standard dictates that we know and do better. He was developing the mind state that I needed him to. We weren't in Disney Land. We were on a level 4 maximum security prison. I knew went you walk with a brother and share jewels (truths) with him the seeds you are planting should eventually take root.

Shortly after that we would come off lockdown and go to the chow hall. They would serve pork on a brunch a menu. Now you might think that's nothing, in prison, it was a big deal. The meals they feed you barely kept you alive, and on the weekend, they went to a two-meal schedule. The CO peeped it first. We just keyed in on it. We stopped the whole chow line, which stopped the morning routine. The OIC[46] was called. He was a character straight from Negro clown school. He was a captain and thought his rank meant something. A lot of them belly crawling Negroes did.

He strutted in and went to the back to talk to the kitchen supervisor. Who must have insured him that was the menu. It was for a regular schedule but not a brunch which was a weekend and holiday menu. He talked his tough talk and left. I found it amusing that these so-called CO's of rank were so stupid.

King walked pass me and go out the line. That was the cue we weren't going to eat anything. All the Gods got out of the line. Then the rest of the pod did except for a few inmates. Some of brothers who had got the pork trays already stopped eating them. We all just sat down peacefully at the tables waiting for

---

[46] Office in Charge

them to open the locked door for we can go back to the pod. But just like that we also found ourselves in a non-violent protest situation because we refused to eat pork.

The Negro inmates were going around like scavengers picking the pork off the left trays. I just observed. My mind shifted to another level of military thinking. I placed points on my mental map where all the Gods and our allies were located. Then I started going down the list and identifying who would be the informants if this elevated. I figured it wouldn't, but you never knew. The only thing we had done was exercise our right peacefully not to eat.

They open the door and we walked back to our pod in silence. We were going to address the situation with the grievance process. When we got back in the CO announced lock into your cells. I had seen this move too many times now. I was a vet. I said if we lock in those cells we are not coming back out and our issue won't be resolved. One brother went to the control booth and got a stack of grievance to pass out. He stated that the CO said we were coming back out. King and I looked at each other and shook our head and smile. The mutual thinking was he was a fool.

Straight out of the VADOC playbook the speakers announced, *"you on lockdown."* The funny thing we would be on lock so much that was like our natural status. I knew what was going to happen next and it did. The Warden, Major, Operation Officers, Investigator, and the OIC all came to our pod. They wanted to know who started this *"organized"* disturbance. They went cell to cell. When they got to us and asked who started it, I said your officer. They couldn't accept the fact that their officer had been the catalyst for this. One of them looked at me like I was a smart ass and kept it moving. The funny thing is they would lock the brother that got the grievance for everybody up and transfer him. They would use him as the scapegoat, label him the instigator, and charge him with an attempt riot. That showed me how the system is designed to disenfranchise prisoners. They could have understood and remedied the situation. They choose to drop a hammer when none was needed. But it was done to strike fear in the rest of the compound. It sent a signal that slaves don't suppose to get out of line.

The rest of the plantation had got pancakes and sausages for brunch and two pieces of chicken for dinner. We never got breakfast and only one piece of chicken at dinner. I guessed that was their way of saying we were bad slaves. Since they didn't want a riot situation on their hand, they corrected the problem. Still, they had to make an example out of us. They kept us on lockdown for two weeks, while the rest of the compound was on regular general population status.

Once again, these mental midgets had failed to seize the moment and do the right thing. They had taken a power position like their moves were infallible. I never expected them to do the right thing when faced with adversity. They had the inability to be men or women of substance.

The lockdowns always provided me with the opportunity to heal from the weight pile. I went hard like most men in prison when lifting weights. I was relieving stress but also pushing the weight of lies, broken promises, and tears that wouldn't drop. It became a refuge and an energy transformation process; despair and misgivings turned into positive nourishment for the muscle. I wouldn't take a hard look at how I worked out until years later. I had got an older cell-partner that was permanently disabled from lifting weights. When I met him, I was irresponsible because I didn't use a spotter. I used to bench and squat 275 pounds by myself. After he shared his story I started to educate myself about the body. The book that would be key in this process was the *Men's Health Home Workout Bible*.

The lockdown provided me with the opportunity to get additional study done. It helped me feed my addiction to knowledge. That was not a bad habit to have. It kept my mind strong. I never wanted to imprison my mind in a steel casket. I looked at that as a slow death. I had observed plenty examples of those that did.

I wrote a lot of letters as well. This was when the five-page back and forth masterpieces came to people by pony express. I remembered the opportunity I had to write one of the God's cousin. She had told me aspects of her story. I was currently studying relationship concepts from a non-Western perspective. I was ready to get a female perspective on polygyny. I knew I laid out a convincing and logic sound augment based on the social conditions dealing with relationship of the day. It took her weeks to respond. I knew she would because I already had caught her mind with my level of conversation. Most women are attracted to intelligent men. Prison allowed me to develop my thinking to new heights.

When she finally wrote and laid down her counter-augment, it was what I thought it would be, predictable. It centered around me fucking another 'bitch.' I had trapped her. She didn't realize it. I responded with that's not the truth since you are having sex with your old boyfriend. Even when he is in a relationship with another woman. I said you just called it "let's keep it on the Down Low." I said what does that do? It's dishonest and made an enemy out of someone who could have been your friend.

Just before we were coming off lockdown, the CO's ran up in designated cells at 3 am with a coordinated strike and drug-sniffing dogs. Her cousin got caught up in that. One of the brothers I was cool with had sent me a kite from the hole stating he got to have the God. That meant he was going to get at him violently. I let him know that can't happen because I only heard one side of the story. Which if it was validate then he had every right to do what he needed to do. The brother that sent the kite was a stand-up dude, tight with me, and held me down in a volatile situation. I knew he wasn't lying.

But protocol dictated I give the God the benefit of the doubt and a chance to respond to a snitch allegation. He never sent word from the hole. While that was going on, his cousin correspondence disappeared as well. It gave creditability to what was being said about him. He got transferred in the process to a medium that was two security levels lower than where we was on. Always a bad way to leave off a compound. It enhanced the probability that he snitched and got rewarded.

All in all, that was the first chance I got to share my developing theory on relationships. Prison breeds a different way of thinking, challenging yourself, and outlook. I learned that I had to question all my concepts on living life and understand the origin of these ideas. They were based on a Eurocentric Judea-Christian construct. I radicalized my thinking by default.

The training of your mind is going to be essential or detrimental to your development. As I rooted myself more deeply in the Nation of Gods and Earths teachings. I refined my behavior to reflect the best of the culture. I also was investigating thinkers and authors that were coming from a Pan-African and Black Nationalism aspect. I think from the age 26-29yrs old I fed my addiction with authors from these schools of thought. I wanted to study other socio-political perspectives and arguments that countered the European worldview as the only standard. I didn't get absorbed into the communist and Arabic Islamic ideas. Although I was familiar with them better than most that had advocated them. I viewed those ideologies as being dangerous for Black Americans. They always seemed to be whitewashed in their historical context. When you study them, the people that advocated it versus their experiences and interaction with African people it always seemed to be lopsided and deceitful.

I felt myself reaching my apex of this prison experience. I did my best not to let doubt creep in. The doubt that I would not go home before 52yrs old. I understood the political landscape, and the climate was still tough on crime. I had to dig deep within myself and work my plan. Mathematics had shown me the numbers. It was unfeasible for the VADOC to keep building prisons. Those like myself that went up for parole would be the safety valve to take the pressure off the system.

You would expect me to understand the political reality, keep my head down, and be invisible. I wish that was my character, but it wasn't. I am holding ciphers on the yard striving to keep the culture of the Nation of Gods and Earths thriving.

Around this time gangs became fashionable in the VADOC. I watched so many Five Percenters turned gang members it was like a pandemic. I was like good because you always should cull the herd of the weak. I understood to be true to this culture you should transform your criminal mentality. A lot of people don't want to do that. Especially when being a *'street nigga'* has become commercialized.

When the VADOC gave the NGE an STG (Security Threat Group) tag, it put constraints on how we moved a little but nothing like the gang label years later would do. We challenged it in a legal suit. I did most of the work. My skill set at the time was weak compared to what it would be the second time I would challenge it. I couldn't prove that they were disadvantaging us according to the U.S. Constitution on that plantation. We were getting all type of 5% literature and able to wear our crowns.[47]The only thing we didn't have was a class. While our legal proceeding was going on the VADOC became concerned about the Bloods. They were becoming entrenched in the system.

The VADOC was trying to associate them in with the Nation of Gods and Earths , which would have brought a different set of problems to address. Then the newfound gang members were crumbling like some cheap prison bread. The investigator was telling them if you say you a Five Percenter we will not send you to the hole if not you are going. The God was sharing this story with us. One of the Bloods told him he did to avoid from going to the hole. I asked him why he didn't straighten it. He looked at me with that coward look on his face. I dismissed him from the table and called the so-called General Blood over. He was a bitch and would eventually be food to them over disloyalty.

I told this pseudo-gangsta what the deal was. I pointed to the coward Blood who tried to taint our name. I let him know straight up that can't happen again. He was looking stupid and said, *"you saying the homey not repping."* I said that's exactly what I am saying because he is standing right there. While Divine

---

[47] The Gods headgear. It has a tassel coming from the center.

who was their Superior use to be a Five Percenter was in the hole. He stormed off like a bitch. Another ranking Blood sat down. I liked him not because he was home team, but because he had a smooth style, and reminded me of a diplomat. He was like they were from different sets, which at the time my educational level on the Bloods was supremely poor. I didn't know what that meant because I always saw them moving together. He apologized for the brother's behavior and gave me assurances that wasn't going to happen again. I said I know. He was fully aware of my disposition on that matter.

The next day on the weight pile the so-called General came to talk to me. That was the last time I saw him ever. Some beef jumped up between them and the GDs. He went to the hole and started upgrading the VADOC information on the Bloods, who didn't know anything. They put a green light on him. But he was a coward before he was Blood. Whoever brought him home didn't check his history on other compounds. If they had done that he would have never been Blood, let alone a general.

The East Coast Bloods would have the VADOC changing policy. If you weren't in a religion, you were a gang member. The Nation of Gods and Earths got labeled a gang. I never saw so many tucked their tail to either denounce being a Five Percenter or to join the gangs who were becoming powerful forces. The funny thing was a lot of ranking members of any gang use to be a Five Percenter. They used always come to our cipher and tell us if we need them they are with us. I always found that interesting. One of my young students at the time would always ask *"why would we need you?"*

We always handled our own.

But as their numbers grew the attitudes of their weaker members became full of hubris. The coward from the previous year who didn't want to own up to being a Blood had a little weight with him now. Too me he was still some dirty little peon. He forgot I was here when the GDs had them under pressure, and for a few weeks you didn't see no Bloods anywhere. At the end of an NOI meeting where I was the guest speaker, he stopped me on our way back to the housing units. And said, *"me and my people took offense to something you said."* I was like what? *"he was like I said it was Islam or nothing. We Bloods and took offense to that."* I said so muthafucking what and kept it pushing. He had a dumb look on his face. He knew I knew he was a coward and he didn't have the juice to call a move that would have started a war.

A few days later at laundry call, I saw him talking to his Superior, who happens to be the highest-ranking Blood on that compound and one of my walking partners around the track. I wanted to show the coward flea how insignificant he was in the grand scheme of things. Soon as I walked up the Superior, he showed me extreme love. I told him I was tempted to smack this flea the other night. He looked at him and made him apologize right there on the spot and then sent him on his way. He looked like a defeated chump. Now and then you must remind people we not the same and fleas have no business trying to fly with Eagles.

That Superior and I walked miles around the track. We had established a good bond which each other. Our relationship came in handy again. When I started to teach a young brother that was leaving the gang life. He was from the Mid-West. The things he saw from his older brother getting killed and his sister getting gang raped then killed; no young person should have endured that. We started out playing chess with each other then it morphed into me teaching him. One day we were going to program, and he was like I am not going. I was like why. Then he told me of the interactions he had with a Blood while in the hole. He was like I just started dealing with the Gods, and I don't want to bring any drama your way. I respected that, but it was unacceptable.

When we went to the program and the Bloods was there. I saw who he was talking about. I was thinking this bitch nigga a Blood; he a snitch. He had ratted on one of my cell partner's nephew giving him life plus 148yrs in prison. Now he a tough guy. I was like when the state clamped down on these gangs a lot of these dudes will never see the streets again. It would be because they took quantity over quality. Life gives lessons that you can't always get back from.

I called over the Superior while we were on the line waiting to get checked and he called over the snitch. I asked did he had any beefs he needed to settle with the young God. He was like I saw he was with ya'll. I let him know anything that happened yesterday was yesterday between them. He agreed it was dead. I didn't know the inner workings of the gang lifestyle, but I knew the streets. So, I always have a heads up. Plus, I didn't fold when I was in them. My character and name were good.

As my time progressed on that compound, I witness a lot of things change. The most disheartening was watching brothers enslave themselves to all the Middle Eastern scholars' rhetoric on Islam. They stop supporting Black American scholars like Warith Deen Muhammad, Elijah Muhammad's son who converted the Nation of Islam to Sunni Islam after he died. These new age Muslims became so out of touch with reality I saw them collectively as a liability. The greatest weakness they had was allowing immature minds to be the Iman of their community if they could read and speak Arab. In prison experience and strong character can keep the peace.

The two things that had etched in my mind about these new Muslims had taken place at the end of Ramadan during the feast. The young Iman wanted to give a speech. You had the NOI, MST, and the Gods in there due to the fact this compound didn't separate the houses like they use to do. This young brother took a shot at every house and showed he lacked experience. The older God that was with us stood up immediately and stop his sermon and challenged him. The inexperience Iman was like, *"who are you their leader?"* The God was like no they are their own leader. They traded points back and forth. The Muslims laughing when they thought this young brother made a point. I looked down the line of Gods, it was maybe 15 of us to about 60 of them. But I looked at those Gods' faces and not a smirk, smile, or laughter could be heard or seen. Everybody's mind had switched to war mode at the same time. I thought to myself if it jumped off, I would be honored to go into battle with these Gods.

The young immature Iman was weak anyway. Word on the compound was his cell partner climbed up onto his bunk and started to grind on him sexually. He did nothing about it. A lot of weak men hid in those religions. But damn for a person to try you like that is the ultimate form of disrespect. The only remedy after that is bloodshed. This was the dude leading the Sunnis. I was thinking at the time of them verbally sparing that if it jumps off this war going to last a long-time and possible carry on other plantations. But shit was in motion, so it had to conclude naturally whether peaceful or not. When we were leaving out the visiting room other houses was like I can't believe he would try to disrespect everybody like that—but they didn't even stand up for themselves. Suckers be everywhere.

I was at a point in my life where I couldn't stomach a lot of these prisoners. They were lost. That revolutionary militant mind was only in a few. It's like religions and gangs were taking over the system and everybody was an alien. Progressive politically and culturally thinkers were on a steady decline. I knew I was at the end of my rope on this plantation. When I witness this Jive Pretender turned Blood. He was said to be a strong teaching of the culture in his hometown. We were all walking back from program, and I asked him a question. He got defensive and flippant. So, I checked him and continued with the conversation. Some might would say I was coming off a little harsh. But I was thinking about all the younger Gods who he had shared knowledge with or directly taught and might think that was the way to go. It wasn't like this dude was in his late teens or early twenties. I always looked at dudes like him unfavorably. They are the ones to lead people into those gangs and trap another generation. The crazy thing is back in the 1960's the Five Percenters taught the gangs out of existence. Those that were enemies were now brothers—that's progressive and community upliftment.

My time on this spot was concluding. I made the process go quicker by signing up for a special food diet which was only carried at a few plantation. Once you are approved, they must ship you.

Almost a year later coming back from the program they called me to the control booth slide me thrash bags. Everyone knew what that meant. I was getting transferred. I went to my cell to pack up. My young student was sad. I think he was like 20 or 21. I was around 30 years old. He used to call me his father because how genuine I use to deal with him. He still didn't let me win in chess though. He sat at my cell door while I packed. I could see a tear fall down his face. I understood because he didn't have any family in the free world. I showed him a standard of brotherhood he never got in the gang life. I wanted nothing from him other than to develop his full potential as a man and a Five Percenter. While others had sort to use him. I taught how to think and make every move his best move. Since he was not finish with his studies under my tutelage, I sent word to another God to take over for he can get his 120 (The Lessons). He was a good young brother. He felt what I and others had felt many times before, nothing last forever in prison. The only thing you can get used to is change. That was the first lesson I had gotten almost 10yrs ago. We had a good solid cadre of Gods up there. He was in good hands. I would miss that cipher of Gods. That was the tightest unit I would be in. I got to see their level of thinking, heart, and brotherhood.

Mountain tour

"The walls, the bars, the guns and the guards
can never encircle or hold down the idea of the people.
Huey Newton

I was a vet at the transfer procedure. I was up when the CO came to my door. The transit process starts from there: Breakfast, property, shackles, bus, central hub, shackles transferred, on a bus to the new plantation.

The destination I thought I was going to I wasn't. Once again, my incompetent counselor had not done her job. It was not surprising. She was too busy shaking her ass and flirting with the male CO's to ever do her job. Now I am heading towards Blue Ridge Mountains to a place called Augusta Correctional Center. Up until that point I was in what was called low lands where most of the prison was staffed by uneducated Blacks. Now I am going to a prison staffed by uneducated and racism Whites. I already knew I was in for an interesting ride.

I knew the vibe up there a little because my C-alike (comrade) was already there. We stayed in heavy conversation through letters. I was privy to the mind state through his observation. I already steeled myself to the racist behavior and draconian policy I would face.

All my property was taken. They were going to go through it with a fine tune comb. Which was interesting because your property gets checked as you pack it on your former plantation. The funny thing it was a comedic character on the ride with me. Any prisoner who would entertain him he asked his question. *"Do they got narcotics up here?"* I laughed to myself because he really thought he was saying some cool shit, by using the word *'narcotics.'* He just was another dope fiend lost in a lifestyle where here felt he had value in. I never talked. I always observed the new surroundings. Anyone can get marked as a victim. I have seen a lot of people get played out of pocket because they didn't heed the first rule of going to a new spot; observe.

I remember this one young dude from Upstate New York coming on a compound I was on. He was on some super friendly and playful shit. One of my brothers/homeboys schooled him that this was not the spot for that. He had no idea what this prison shit produced in some males. Until one of his wrestling partners tried to fuck him. He had to fight for his manhood. When we saw him on the yard, we just looked at him like I told you so. How people perceive you is based off how you carry yourself from the first moment you hit the compound.

When I went to property to get my stuff after these CO's inventory it. I saw my Universal Flag (the same symbol they would consider gang-related later) on top that had my name on it in the allowed property stack. I didn't even check the rest of it. I would deduce what I couldn't have by what I had. My Walkman which was brought off the yard and a taped-up *Enemies Clashes of the Races.* I loved that book.

Word on the yard was they were hard on Five Percenters here. They had already disenfranchised us before it became policy. I suspected it had to do with a power dynamic and brothers not showing and proving righteous behavior.

I had a decade in prison all done on maximum security. I was well-seasoned to the prison bullshit and respected first as a man and then a Five Percenter. I went about my day like I usually do. After doing enough time your routine stays the same. You run into people that you bided with on other spots. You lose respect for some of them as well. I remember this faux Muslim. He was the Nation of Islam student minister on the last spot. When I got to this plantation one of my brothers was like he just left and had turned back into a flaming homosexually. I would have loved to hear his reasoning on why he started to take the dick again. He used to try to chastise me and another God on some moralist tip because we use to smoke weed. I used to tell him I am righteous, not holy.

Weak people hide in religions, gangs, and different currents of thinking. A main reason it took me a while to open up to anyone beyond a surface level. But a lot of time you can spot that grade of character quick. Who you are at the core doesn't change. It's like your operating system. Everything else you embrace is the software. You should be a man first before you accept any lifestyle. I never got swept up into that brotherhood concept just because you claim the same ideas as me. My experiences and snitches gave me another set of tools to exam a man's character with. I have seen a lot of good brothers fall time and time again behind these marshmallow centered dudes.

The men I bonded with vibrated on the same frequency I did. I was never dogmatic or a zealot about being a Five Percenter. This was a lifestyle choice I chose. I didn't build walls around me. I did lean more towards men that were knowledgeable about the Global Black experience and applied it to their lives. I had a more lenient understanding with people younger than me. The reason why was when I was younger it was an older brother I use to walk the yard with. He had stated to me, *"I only owe one jewel to a person younger than me either they grasp it, or they don't. But a person older than me I owe them nothing."*

The activity from the Five Percenters on this compound was invisible by the time I got there. I had got me an update from King on where the culture stood now, who was who, and what he had done to get things going. We had already been on two compounds (this would be our third). He had got Knowledge of Self amongst a good cadre of Gods that were disciplined, militant, and knew what brotherhood really meant.

I told him to call a Universal Cipher.[48] I was surprised at the number of Gods that showed up. They had at least 3 times the amount that we had on the last compound. I asked a few questions and let them build on the state of the culture there. All I heard was fear! That shit always silently enraged me. When I heard enough, I stepped into the middle of the cipher and started building on who we supposed to be. If you are not carrying it like that, you are not my A-alike. I let them know Allah don't hide under rocks and what did they expect from a CO populace raised in the mountains? I could see in their eyes a lot of them didn't

---

[48] A mandatory meeting amongst the Five Percenters.

take to kindly to my words, but I didn't give a fuck. One thing I learned through misfortune is you don't let weak people stay amongst your ranks.

The primary standard I uphold is you must be a man first. You can embrace all the ideologies you want but if you are not principle strong and unwavering in the face of adversity; then you are a coward. Weaklings should not be allowed to stand amongst men. I walked away from that cipher. I already knew this was going to be a challenging spot for me. I didn't know now but would find out later that the VADOC was fading out the STG[49] tag and classifying everyone as a gang member. As well putting us in databases. I would be looked at as a leader in the Nation of Gods and Earths. I wasn't because we had no leaders. I just had magnetism based on my stance within the culture.

I used to be up early mornings thinking, that's when emotions would hit me. The main thing was the extreme loneliness I felt. I like most people wore the mask of indifference like nothing bothered or phased me. But alone to my own thoughts, I was vulnerable and exposed. I had to kill these feelings in darkness like one pluck out weeds from their garden. I was a passionate person who had to be cold-hearted. That was a duality of self. I missed the tenderness, softness, and wetness of women. I knew I had at least 10 to 15 more years to do before I made parole. I was under no illusion about my possibility with women. I didn't mess with the female CO's or staff and being gay didn't even register in my mind. I considered myself a man that live by G-codes, warrior codes, and Five Percent tenets. So, no male could be considered a female in my eyes.

A deeper thought that bothered me at times was I didn't have any children. I thought about when I was younger the two sisters that had abortions. During those moments, I realized how my stance on abortion had changed. It from a nonchalant approach like whatever you decide I am alright with it too I am not with it at all. I am not talking about in extreme cases of rape,

---

[49] STG is a security threat group. It is what VADOCs label any group, organization, or culture that doesn't promote sheep ideology.

incest, or the health of the mother is in jeopardy. I didn't regret much of the things I did in my life. But I did regret that. Children are our greatest wealth, resource, and legacy.

When the morning whistle for count time blew, it was back to the iron mask. It's funny how dishonest one becomes to himself. It's a safety measure because if you express your true emotional range, then predators will look at you as weak. They will try to apply con game on you or others will try to move on you on some homosexual shit. Then you will only be left with one option as a man. The level of inhumanness you developed won't be fully known until you get back into society. It's a tradeoff for the strength you gain versus the emotions you lose. The hidden secret was you must put this mask on every day. You can't take a day off. You live in a state of hyper-alertness and you must be prepared to react to anything in a nanosecond. I knew I couldn't live in prison and society at the same time.

The only time I felt like a human and could be at ease was when my family came to see me. Which was when I requested it, usually like every 2-3 years. It was when I couldn't take being in prison anymore. I needed familiarity with people who knew who I use to be. My family lived out-of-state. They had to use their vacation time to come see me for a whole weekend. I couldn't be selfish and request this every year. I asked the least as possible from my family. I created this situation and felt I had to thug it out. This was my tribulation. I had to go through it to discover who I was.

I didn't have any more women to write or was pressed to meet anyone. I learned women want to hear true lies or think they are going to treat you anyway because you are locked up. I specialized in sending them their pictures and letters. I didn't give a fuck. My mind had totally shifted to doing time and nothing else. Plus, what could I write a woman and it be what she wanted to hear? All I did was read, discussed what I read, and worked out. I knew the caliber person I was. I wasn't going accepted a subpar woman because of my conditions. I couldn't lie to women for snack money, letters, or visits. Since I couldn't interact with the type of women I liked, I just shut down to the possibility of dealing with women. No emotional attachments.

The longer I was incarcerated humanity was seeping out of me. I became apathetic to my present reality. Women really do balance men out. All I had was my brotherhood and theories on how I would act when I was released. I knew I had transformed my criminal mentality to a progressive one. But I didn't know how that would look in society. All I knew was what I wasn't into anymore. I had a vision of the man I wanted to be at the end of my incarceration. I was taking steps to be that person. By this time, I had a decade of living the concept that *"Blackman is God"* and there is no mystery god in the sky. I created my own hell by playing into the traps that were set for me. I knew when the chance revealed itself I would create my own heaven.

As I did my time on this spot my disdain grew. It is hard not to become militant minded in harsh condition. They ran this level 3 like a level 5 or 6 prison. I had came from a level 4. The CO's just pushed and harassed you when left or enter the building. Then a few of them had reckless mouths. They were cold cowards. But who wanted another 5 or 10 years for whipping a CO's ass. Then one evening a CO that push to much bullshit got beat-up by a homosexually. He was the joke of the plantation. It was good to see him with a black eye.

I really understood what racism looked like amongst the most ignorant white people with authority. I knew this was the same class of people that rich landowners used during slavery as slave breakers, overseers, and paddy rollers. The funny thing was this prison staff was predominately white, and you could count the Black staff on one hand, and that included the warden. Rumor had it when the warden was a major here they set his car on fire. Word was he had a weak dick for white women. My observation of him confirmed that. He had that old 70's Negro player's vibe.

But to his credit, he didn't play that racism thing. I remember one Sunday, I was in my cell studying while the pod was watching sports. Sports is big in prison. The pod got dangerously quiet. I knew something was up. When I came out my cell, a few of the white prisoners were steaming. One of them was like the CO in the booth told the floor officer to *"tell those two monkeys to stop working out."* She was refereeing to two young Gods that was in the pod with me.

The floor officer assessed the vibe and knew his coworker had fucked up. I already knew how to get things done in our favor. I told the floor office to call the OIC (officer in charge). He knew he had a potential riot situation on his hands. To me, it wasn't that serious, but still, I wanted the racist CO to realize we were not monkeys or completely powerless. Then I had the two young Gods call their families, tell them to call up here, complain today and Monday to the warden's office. I learned to use the same system to fight them how they fight us.

The booth officer who was a mean, old, drunk white lady. She immediately came to the floor apologizing. She knew she had fucked up too. We all knew we were on a racially charged plantation. And a spark could really set it off. We still executed our moves. The warden would censure and suspend her. I had learned over the years, at times, the feather is just as strong as the hammer. You don't always have to get violent to move levers to get the response you want. You could never win in a violent altercation with the VADOC. That momentarily satisfaction is going have a devastating impact on you. For starters, they have an arsenal at their disposal. No matter how big your prison shank, it can't beat a shotgun.

The sad thing was you had Negros be like that was fucked upset she got suspended. She a good CO some of them said. I thought damn these niggers are fucked up. A person that would call a Black man a monkey, they empathized with. While we had white prisoners ready to tear shit up if we had encouraged it. When she would die some months later, these same clowns were expressing remorse. Times like this I could really imagine what it must have been like for the strong-willed people that were in slavery having to deal with this weak traitorous breed.

My ancestral memories used to shoot through my synapses and share visions with me. I always wonder what made some breed of men weak and comfortable living on their knees. I had around 13 years in prison now, and my disdain was still growing. I felt it was a time bomb ticking in me. I really didn't know how much more of the bullshit I could endure. I started getting deeper into meditation and Qigong practices. I had found a Qi-gong book in the library. It had around 3 to 4 styles in it. I had settled on the 8 brocades because it looked the least martial. If the CO's saw you doing katas on the yard, they immediately stop you.

On the worst compound I would find my greatest jewel. That opened my mind up to studying different Eastern philosophies. I already had study Eastern history, so this would complement that.

Still in the Mts

"Nothing about 'Brotherhood'
is ever wrapped up in a nice package."
Annabeth Gish

I started to see the sway the gang ideology was having on the younger prisoners. It was a fad now. I knew that eventually policymakers were going to crack down on these cats. I couldn't see the purpose of joining a gang in prison. Sure, it was violent at times, but you still could navigate your way without a gang. I just saw most of them young cats wanting to be down with something greater than themselves. They would learn over time nothing is free.

It started to be a disproportion number of dudes from NY claiming Blood. I used to laugh when they use to tell me you can come home and be a Captain or starred General. It was always the younger ones with rank who said this. But those who were in my peer group never fixed their mouth to say that. They knew from my style of man and being a true Five Percenter; it wasn't a chance in hell. I kept meeting a lot of I use-to-be Five Percenters who were Bloods. I used to debrief them on the why. I stopped debriefing them. I got tired of hearing the flimsy excuses that made no sense.

A lot of the NY dudes claiming Blood wasn't as official to me as they thought. Sometimes when I was walking the track, they would call me over to get my opinion on some home team nonsense. They were checking each other. But when I heard they didn't know little shit like Albee Square Mall had turned into Fulton Mall, this was before I left in 1995. They didn't know Malcolm X Blvd used to be Utica Ave, or never heard of the clubs Homebase or The Muse. They didn't know the Limelight Club was housed in a church. They all fell under suspicion to me. I didn't play the homeboy shit anyway. I left them to their New York dreams. They came off as wannabes.

It was one young Blood who I took a likening too. I used to snatch him up to walk the track with me. He didn't have much, and his crew treated him like he was bothersome. I knew their level of brotherhood was fake. You never kick a man when he down or make him beg you for anything. I was working at the shoe shop. I asked one of the older brothers I knew to get him a job. I did that for he didn't have to keep his hand out to his so-called brothers. I always looked at the person trying to embarrass another person in front of others as weak.

Once he started working with me, we use to eat lunch together every day. He told me his story. It was a heartfelt one, from being homeless to being kidnapped. I could see why some of these young dudes turn to gangs. Sometimes that was all they had. During one lunch session, he was like you know a lot of the NY home team don't like you. He was naming names of the ones that spoke to me the most. I found that amusing. He was like they use to tell him don't walk the track with me because I was on that *"Godbody shit hard."* That I was going to try to turn him into a Five Percenter. I found that funny as well. But the young brother was like *"I can see now the reason they didn't like you because you are a man."* At that moment, I realized I crossed a barrier in his mind of genuineness. Then it hit me that most younger brothers truly have not met men that are solid and principle strong.

I was the first person he had met that didn't try to use or belittle him for having nothing. I encouraged him to be a better him. Whether it was taking my time out to talk to him, provide a job for him, or encouraged him to participate in the Pan-African class. That was a good feeling to show a younger brother a different model of manhood. That you didn't have to stay in a criminal mentality. There was no dishonor in seeking the best you. There is a principle that unalike attract. I had just witnessed it in real-time. I was paying the real debt that I owed. It was fishing these young brothers out of a cesspool and giving them the tools to make different choices.

At the same time, I was talking to another young Blood and encouraged him to start buying books on the Black experience. He was just like countless others who swear they were founded by the original Black Panther Party. I considered myself a student of the Black Panther Party movement. I studied them because the government destroyed them with every dirty trick you could think of. That was a reoccurring theme in the Black experience in this country. Whether it was bombing self-sufficient business areas like Black Wall St to dropping bombs on the Move movement family house. Black people are seen as threats in this country and pseudo-citizens.

I used the Black Panther angle to try to transform the brother criminal thinking into one of a progressive thinker on socio-political issues. I never talked down about the Bloods. I did point out what he lost versus what he gained, which was nothing, but 15 years in prison. He was out there being a father to his children and had a common-law wife. He was one of the few Bloods that I would meet that was thorough and was locked-up for some gang-related business. He was official.

As we walked the yard, I would recommend books for him to read to expand his thinking. I suggested he build his own library. Which he did. I told him to get *Black Man, Obsolete, Single, and Dangerous* by Haki Madhubuti. I am a huge fan of Haki works because it's aggressive and raw. That book I considered the Blackman's bible.

We were walking the yard one day and he informed me he was moving to the non-smoking pod. That's where I was with a few of my cadre members. I figured he wanted to get down with how we studied, even though we had a Sunday study group on the yard. He knew we had a daily one in the pod. We kept the tradition of prison being an institution of higher learning alive.

I knew this Blood for well over a year before he decided that he didn't want to bang anymore and become a Five Percenter. He chose to walk the yard by himself for a few months after he dropped his flag, so he can handle what drama came with that. I respected that he wasn't trying to duck any penalty. At the end of the day, you have to be a man before you be anything.

Once his business was finished however it was, I became his educator in the teachings of the Nation of Gods and Earths (NGE). My personality switched towards him because of how serious I took the teachings. The protocol of memorizing 120 especially when you were a poor student is overwhelming to most. He was no different. I also knew when you teach non-mainstream teaching centered on awakening the God within you become a target (threat). They assassinated the founder of the NGE, Allah the Father, because he woke the youth up to their true potential. Everybody fears the potential in Black people, but what former slave owners feared the most is, are we going to do to them what they have done to us for centuries.

He used to complain about the work. I let him know exercising and developing your mind is the key to greatness. He was like nobody expected much from him. My thing was to get him to think critically. Once he understood his mind could be strengthened, then everything went easy. It takes a different discipline to work on yourself internally.

When people viewed our cadre from outside, they just saw the strength and discipline. But when they got inside, they learn it was hard work. The hours of study, exchanging of ideas, and working out made us sharp and aware. Since I was the older brother I got to hear their personal stories. This was when the real transformation took place. We all are a sum of the experiences we gained from our choices. One thing I use to advocate is not to be a slave to a feeling that came from a bad experience. I was like you must learn from it and let it go, or it will consume you. I used the example of the rat cowards who testified on me. I said I didn't allow that to hinder me from meeting good people. But I did take a lesson from it.

Now the former Blood was doing good, building a stronger relationship with his mother and the mother of his children. He was growing. Then one day a new Blood came on the compound supposed to be a 4-star general. He inquired about him, and another God on his side of the yard was like he wanted to meet. He was one of them use to be Five Percenters that turned Blood.

We meet that Saturday on the fence. I listened to questions he was asking the young God. His tone turned me off. Especially when he was talking what was supposed to happen to him when he left. I let him know right then this man walked the yard by himself and nobody served no penalty on him. Now that he was God that's not going to happen at all. It's going to be what it's going to be. I turned to young God and told him you don't have to burn yourself. They had some protocol that you suppose to burn off what they called a dog paw.

Shit got tense, but when I am with you, I am with you. The young God looked at me and then at the other Gods that was around. He knew we had his back and we were comfortable with whatever choice he made. He chose to get the burn. We all left in peace. As we walked off the young God said, *"Didn't you just go up for parole the other day?"* He was letting me know with that question he had thought it through critically and made the best decision for everybody. He was learning what real brotherhood should be. You don't push the button because you can. He realized even in a win it's going to be a lot of losers.

The sad thing is that it's more stand-up men in prison than on the streets. Every so often I was reminded of that. It shows when you are in the moment. I like to say in real-time. When certain codes/principles are a part of you, you don't have to second guess yourself. It's that reason I became more selective with who I bonded with. I realized I had an aspect of my personality that was still ride or die if I dealt with you. I felt no need to weed that out. Only to refine the process of bond building. Everybody is not capable or worthy of that exchange of loyalty.

Serious Nature of the Crime

Another turned down!

I knew I wasn't going to make parole in my early 30's. It was no reason why. They still were building prisons. It was people with drug charges or offenses less than murder who were still eligible for parole. It was a hard pill to swallow knowing the whole process was a sham. I knew people that stop participating in it. I figured I have nothing to lose by still going up for parole. And since I didn't have an infraction since I was 26yrs old, the process became political. The parole board was acting like a judicial body and with each turndown I became indifferent. It didn't faze me. That started to worry me a little bit. I knew from an intellectual standpoint I was becoming more disconnected from the human element in myself. I knew it was a defense mechanism. I remembered my first few months in the big house. A gentleman hung himself because he had got his 18th turndown for parole. I had seen them cart the body out. I had wondered at the time what level of hopelessness he was feeling to take his own life.

I recognized who I was historical inside of this American tragedy. I played into their trap, and this was my penalty. You can't use the snake deck of cards and think you are going to win. He operates from a different archetype.

I seldom thought about the streets now. My letters came infrequently, but they still came. I was always grateful for that. It was still those that took a moment out of their day to think about me after all this time had passed. It made me reflect even further on the man I used to be versus the man I was at that moment. I knew one thing for sure, the love I was being shown was not on par with the friendship I had given. I had put it on the line for people countless of times; whether it was beef, moral support, or money. And now to barely get a letter was an interesting turn of events for me. I used to be one of the first checked, now I suspected, I barely registered as a whispered thought in a drinking or a smoke session.

I was alone. I accepted my downfall and everything that came with it. That's why I never fold. When false promises of freedom were offered for my integrity to betray my main man I didn't even register it. I knew I was doing a different type of bid. I suffered in silence. I always thought the strongest commodity men had was brotherhood. I guess I was just coming from a stand-up man perspective. I was surprised at the number of masks that fell off people faces. I didn't become cold-hearted or destructive to myself. I just learned the lesson from what was revealed.

When I was into rhyming I had, a song called *'Real Niggas is a Dying Breed.'* My pain and true thoughts I used to write in rhymes. I always wrote from a soulful to blues perspective. *'Life ain't Fare'* was another song I was working on in the studio at the time of my incarceration. Pain is a real experience. But to swallow that pain and make it fuel is another way I survived. I didn't turn inward or lash out at people. I learned to cope. I still wonder what level of humanity was left in me.

I was being cheated out of experiencing my full emotional range. The age I was at I should have been a father and husband, but I wasn't. I wasn't anything. I wasn't even the real me. I was a shadow of myself, and I knew it. While others saw a razor-sharp thinker, discipline, militant Blackman, that was my armor to house and protect the one ounce of passion, compassion, and vulnerability that I had left in me. I am a good-hearted person by nature. I wanted to see the best in a person. But life showed me I couldn't fully invest in that type of thinking. And prison showed me you couldn't be a real human in Hades. How can you when you on hyper-alert status for danger even when you sleep?

Seconds passed into minutes, minutes into hours, hours into days, days into months, months into years, and I did the same thing every day. If it weren't for books, magazines, and PBS, I would have gone crazy. I kept fueling my mind. I could liberate it from the limited confinements of my incarcerated body. I saw the beauty pass this hellhole. The biggest trick is to trap your mind then you become an institutionalized slave. I never forgot what living outside a razor fence felt like. I never forgot the good memories I had going to family events or dealing with women. I knew this was a leg of my journey. The most painful one.

One morning I came back off the yard from working out, I see my cell door open, and lights on. The Negro inmate sitting in the dayroom gave me a look. I knew the CO's was in my cell shaking it down. I couldn't figure out why? I didn't involve myself in any criminal activity or use drugs. I stayed in my own lane.

I watched how the old lady CO watched me when I entered the pod. Her eyes followed me all the way to my cell. I knew she was wondering how I was going to respond. My daily movement was discipline, courtesy, and respectful. When you move with a high level of self-control, you really become a target. The VADOC doesn't look at you like a regular prisoner because you don't fit their profile of what is considered prison normal.

I got to my cell and saw these two pink CO's had thrashed my cell. It looked like a hurricane came through there. For one second, I lost my cool and snapped. I was disappointed in myself that I had let this lesser man and mental midget tick me off. The sergeant had the nerve to ask me why I am talking to them in that tone and manner, we not disrespecting you. It took everything in my power not to kick him in his pink face. I saw my creative work, personal research, and inner thoughts scattered everywhere. I asked why you didn't call me off the yard for I could be present when you are shaking my cell down. I knew of stories where CO's planted drugs or a banger in a person's cells. He responded we didn't have to if a sergeant present. I wanted to spit in his face. This was the first prison where I wasn't present for a shakedown.

I knew what they were looking for. I said I could have saved you the trouble. Then went through the proper channels to get the Lessons back. They used to take my Five Percent Newspaper ever shakedown. I would go to property, show my property slip, and get them back.

They took some of the Lessons and a few of my poems but left a complete set of 120. I knew these dummies didn't know what they were looking for. They left leaving me with their mess to clean up. I thought what had change that warrant this. I would come to find out that after being a decade in prison now this was considered gang contraband.

My cell-door shook it was the control booth officer. She had a pass for me to go to the investigator's office. She was like why are they bothering you? I told her because I was a Five Percenter. She looked like really, then said you been that since you been here, which was around 3yrs. That let me know they were watching me since I been on the compound. I got my pass and went to see the investigator.

Now the interesting thing about the investigator, she was the property office when I first arrived at this cuckoo's nest. Our conversation was interesting because I didn't fear the administration. As our conversation unfolded, I told her everything I have you gave it to me when I transferred here. She said, *"I know, but the status of the Five Percenters changed to a gang."* I was like if that was so where is the memo stating that, especial for those of us who were in the system when we weren't labeled a gang? When policy change, a memo is supposed to come out informing you of that change. I asked how could I be in *"compliance"* with the rules if I don't know them? Make a long story short I never saw any memo. She was like her partner wanted to give me a gang-related charge, but she talked him out of it. I saw through her angle. I let her know if I did get a charged I would fight it all the way to federal court.

Her face telegraphed who this nigger thinks he is. I am sitting up in her office relaxed with my legs crossed on some 'G' shit. I didn't have that inherent fear most prisoners had when dealing with them. If was always a chance you could go to the hole from here. The investigator word was like gold to her higher-ups. She had told me about her trip to South Africa trying to bond with me. I just listened looking at her blonde hair and blue eyes and thinking you look just a Boer. As I was exiting she told me I should clean up my cell because any Five Percenter material I get caught with moving forward I will be charged as a gang member.

I talked to a few Gods who were in my inner cipher. I explained what went down. They were like what's the next move. I considered filing another lawsuit, but I decided against it for two reasons at that time. One was I felt that a lot of Gods had too much fear in their hearts. They were scared to be open and proud Five Percenters. They needed to feel what real pressure felt like. That living a non-mainstream ideology birth in the Black experience at times have blowback from slave makers. Another reason was I knew this was just the beginning. From what I observed about the VADOC, I knew they would keep pushing policies that would put me in a better position tomorrow to file a stronger lawsuit.

I knew I wasn't going home no time soon. I was waiting like Michael Meyers. The thing that would always show me the diabolic nature of this mental midgets was they knew we weren't a gang. I was told this to my face on multiple occasions. But lower-level pawns that saw a way to advance in their careers off the backs of mislabeling a group of prisoners. These imps rose in stature and rank. They would eventually get their own gang unit that roamed around the state doing a bunch of fake shit. I used to laugh at them. They even had their own uniforms and symbols.

What made it worst was the leader of the gang unit was from NYC, so he knew the history of the Nation of Gods and Earths. He was a sucker. It was buzz that a prisoner was fucking his wife and usually those types of rumors are true. The prison grapevine is almost efficient as the internet.

Get use to nothing

In these mountains, you had Caucasian prisoners calling themselves Jungle Aryans. I had never seen so many thunderbolts and 88s tattoos in my life. They were bold and knew things favored them. I wondered how many of them were sissies on low-land.[50]These Aryans were planning an escaped that was supposed to take place during graduation. They were going to take people family members hostage. While a crew of them begin stabbing Black prisoners on the yard for a diversion. But one of them got chicken-hearted and spilled the beans. We knew something had happened because soon as we got to work, they blew the whistle for us to go back to our buildings for a count.

Once everybody was locked in their cells, we could see the CO's on the yard with metal detectors. The yard was one of the better places to stash bangers because if they find it, it's in a common area. And they found a lot that day.

All I cared about was will my visitors be let in this weekend, because there wasn't any way I could warn them. Prison has a policy that once it goes on the lock you don't get to use the phone or take a shower for 3 days. But I was supposed to be being rehabilitated. Everything I would witness let me understand that prison is a cattle business. We were just an income-driven investment.

I didn't want to go crazy in prison like I would see other people do over the years. The official response is to pump you up with drugs. I took every measure to help discipline my mind. The longer I did time in prison the longer I would see the medication line grow. I was convinced they had to be experimenting on these men. It's not like they have not done it before.

When you in prison your jailers like to think you are expendable. Therefore, outside support is a must. I have seen men die or severely injured due to neglect from the medical staff. One of the reasons, I switch my diet to what they called common fare.[51] I figured if I stay healthy, out the pill line, I could stay alive and walk out of prison.

The prison environment was changing for the worst. Stand-up men started to become less and less. A small portion of young dudes floated to the homosexually current. Just enough that it

---

[50] The name was given to prisons, not in the mountains.
[51] Which was mainly raw fruits, vegetables, peanut butter/ jelly, tuna, sardines, and 3 hot meal entrees a week.

was noticeable that this was a different breed. I figured most of them was closet gays on the streets.

The gangs were getting a bigger foot hole. I knew it was a matter of time before the VADOC become more reactionary to them. And they did. They used to round them up in lots and ship them to the supermax on some preemptive strike. I knew the young gang members didn't understand the politics of prison. The extreme conditions they were being sent to would radicalize a few or break all of them.

The Arab styled, and interpretation of Islam started to become move prevalent. I saw that as another slave making tool. I remembered a book I had read called *From Niggas to Gods*. It had a chapter about people going from slaves to whites under Christianity to slaves to Arabs under Islam. I knew whether you were a gang member or zealot if you didn't know yourself and people history then you can only be a slave to someone else cause. Arabs have never shown any brotherhood to Black people.

I take hard stances because life showed me it's not fair. So, to be naïve or stupid on top of that is a dangerous combination. Once you know different histories breed different mentalities in people (cultures), then you can deal with them accordingly. I understood it is easy for some to be a slave than a free man.

The worst part of being in prison is bonding with a good dude then see that person make a move that's going to get him more time. Then you remember we still in prison and a person got to be a man first. Men live by certain codes and when it's violated I''s going to be bloodshed.

I tried to talk a brother out of doing something because he was working on his freedom. But how he was going about it was trying to raise funds for a lawyer by selling weed. You might think that is stupid, but you didn't have 90 years with no parole. I learned not to judge another man's action because I didn't have his burden. He had the compound on lock. I am one of the few people that knew that. He kept his separation from the hand to hand stuff. He went through another brother (strawman) who had lost respect in real dude's eyes. He involved himself in a homosexual relationship and fell in love with a white boy. He was the go-between in the transaction. The other person thought he was dealing with the strawman.

I guess the other dude decide to let greed and his lack of respect for the middleman be his motivating factor for keeping the pack. People usually make wrong choices that come with serve consequences.

When I came from morning yard call to check my man. I saw what he was doing, and his eyes told me the rest. I still tried to talk him out of it. He was like nobody going to take anything from me. I was like he doesn't know it's your pack. He was like you know the rules. And kept doing what he was doing. I did know the rules because we were peers, the same age, and from the same class that entered prison in 1995. I chose to lay down that element in myself because I knew the rules. I wanted to get out of prison one day and knew I couldn't take another jury trial. I would have felt dishonest to let the state kill me with a lethal injection.

I often wonder why I was able to see the direction the street mentality was going and started to work on transforming the more detrimental aspects of it. I knew in my heart I couldn't live by those codes anymore because my lost had been too great. There are no part-time gangsters. When you in you all the way in. If I was still in did then I would have been obligated to get busy with my man. I was out and watching him make a banger. I locked in for count knowing in a few hours the whole compound going to be on lockdown.

He called me to the door after the CO's counted and left. He was like you feel me. I was like no. I was like in this game you take losses. This loss should be on the other cat. He was responsible for making sure that pack hit and was secure. It's his battle, not yours. He should be on the hook for the money. He didn't see my reasoning. All he saw was somebody took something from his surrogate, so he took it from him.

What's set in motion now had to play out. I did my job as a confidant and adviser.

Yard

I am walking the yard with my young shadow. I updated him on what was about to go down. The first thing he asked me did you tried to talk him out it. See the other brother was a good brother who people respected and admired. Nobody wanted to see the brother get more time or the death penalty. But I understood his position even though I disagreed with it. It's hard for some to transform a mentality that comes naturally to them. This brother was extremely advanced in his thinking and highly educated in the socio-political reality of the Black American experience, but he was forced to stay in a street mentality to raise money for a lawyer.

We walked the yard, it was an extremely nice Sunday. It was a softball game going on. In prison, they sponsor tournaments all year around softball, soccer, basketball, volleyball, and boxing. They recognize we still must have outlets to release our energy and fellowship. But if a group of us get together to exchange ideas, they break that up. They fear the cultivation of the mind, but not playing sports.

I watched as my man approached the dude with the straw-man. The dude brushed it off. He was coaching his team. I knew he had made a mistake. Had he stepped away and conducted business the stabbing probably could have been avoided. He didn't see it coming. He should have known it was going to be repercussion for taking a person's pack. He strived to fight back, but it was too late. He was leaking from his face. The yard scattered.

The assailant got swallowed up in the crowd and was able to switch his blood pattern shirt. The level of camaraderie in prison is on another level. It was the convict code. All this was done in minutes because the yard got shut down immediately with no movement. The VADOC protocol is to inspect us one at a time as we trickle back into the building. They were looking for signs of who was in the altercation.

I knew everyone involved would be identified from the human cameras. The VADOC informant network is about as good as the FBI's Top Echelon Program. When they had got the strawman, I knew the dude who was playing tough told. The middleman didn't do a thing on the yard but had a simple look on his face. He always told stories about how he got busy on different compounds. He was disillusion. His hoe card got pulled. Men in prison don't do shady business with dudes they know it's going be problems with. Even if they can handle them.

We were locked in our cells for hours, and my man was like *"yo you think I got away."* I was like no. He was like you right, and 15 minutes later they came and got him. That was the last time I saw him. Prison is so unstable because its filled with people, run by people, and you never know what a person is going to do, especially in close-quarters.

Knowledge Group

I was saturated with Black ideology and moved like a non-slave and that use to bother a lot of the white administration on this plantation. I used to get books denied. But the one highlight of being on this compound was they had a Pan-African class called the Knowledge Group. The one flaw was the two people in charge was homosexuals, but even more wild, they were members of the Moorish Science Temple of America (MSTA). I didn't even try to understand how they rationalized all of that. I wasn't homophobic, but I still wondered how they worked those conflicting ideologies out. They were good people though.

One of them I use to have good conversation with on various subject. So, one day at chow I asked him about his sexual orientation. He told me he was married at one-time and in the military. While in the military it was a click from the major cities and they had an undercover lifestyle. That an older NYC fella had turned him out. He had paused for a minute when another gay dude walked by. They had been into a few fights. I thought to myself what do these punks have to fight about. He then told me in the gay world they have different houses. I silently laughed because it sounded like some vampire shit with different covenants. I think I had watched Blade to many times because that was my point of reference.

The brother was extremely knowledgeable about Pan-African history. He would later get transferred because him and the other gay dude kept battling each other.

His co-chair and fellow Moor took over the class. I didn't know he was gay at first. Then I heard dudes call him Swiss roll like the Little Debbie cakes and referred to him as a shark. They called him shark because he circles around young white boy that hit the plantation. The Swiss roll moniker came from because he liked to eat Swiss roll cakes out of ass-holes. I knew right then that this fella was sick. He wasn't the first inmate that I met that was sick. He walked proudly of his station in the gay world. I thought it was fucked up because he was one of the few faces of the MSTA on that compound.

He would eventually leave the Knowledge Group. I became the chairman. I was always teaching the class anyway. The numbers had increased when I started teaching. If you weren't into religion and wanted to learn from a Black frame of reference you came there.

The administration had gutted all the programs resources by taking the lockers that stored books and videos for each group. Their reason was that a group of Caucasians in the Odin religion had slaughtered the group leader in their class. They had the bangers stashed in their locker. The VADOC claimed it was a ritual sacrifice and that's what made the newspapers. But one of the older Five Percenters that knew him said it was bullshit. That he was killed because a crew of Aryans tried to take over the group. They wanted to enforce a policy that no Blacks should be allowed to come.

After that, no group had a resource locker. A staff member had to sit in and monitored the classes. It was one lady that kept writing reports on me. That lead me to get censured and then suspended from the class for a month. The Caucasian lady warned me and wrote me up twice about using *"harsh language."* I ignored Ms. Piggy. The real reason was I had checked dudes coming to our class flirting with her. Some Negros think every white woman is a beauty queen. I told her I am talking to men if you don't like what I have to say then tell them to put someone else. When my counselor who was a White man used to sit in there, he never had a problem. He used to look forward to our one on one counseling visits just to talk to me about whatever I was teaching on. I knew the difference wasn't because he was a man but a Northerner.

One day I was summoned to get my parole answer, which was a turndown—no surprise there. As I was walking off the lady was like did you get this paperwork. I stopped and like what paperwork. She handed me a month suspension from the Knowledge Group. I looked at her like she was crazy. I wanted to smack that smug look off her face. I never heard of anyone getting suspended from any religion or cultural program. And the reason was that I used harsh language. It highlighted the word *"faggot."* I didn't recall saying it, but I probably did and so what.

That fat stubby pig had written me up again. I had told her before I talk like I wanted to. I am talking to Black men and this the tone I am coming in. I didn't give one flying fuck about how she felt about it. I didn't find her desirable like the coons.

I wasn't even mad about getting another parole turn-down, but I was about getting suspended from the Knowledge Group. That was my lifeline. I enjoyed sharing ideas in an organized manner and stimulating the minds of my people. One young brother was from Sierra Leone. He was like I learned more about my country and Africa from this group then I did back home. That was the greatest reward a teacher of truth can receive.

I knew they thought by systemically removing me they would kill our numbers. They didn't realize the class was set-up from a collective teaching style. It was still great builders (teachers) in the group.

But that blow still hit me, because I enjoyed fellowshipping from a cultural standpoint with different brothers. I would prepare for hours it was my meditation time.

All they were trying to do was to break my spirit, control me, and show me they are powerful on this poor part of the planet. It did the opposite. It just validated what I already knew. A strong Black man is perceived as problem to white people no matter if the power dynamic favored them.

karma is funny. Her husband got escorted off the compound by CO's because he got caught sucking an inmate's dick. Imagine that! I was relishing in her embarrassment. When she saw me, she knew it. I didn't try to hide the smirk. That was the second time within a 10-year period that a male staff member would get escorted off for engaging in homosexual activity. Every prison I had been on female CO's and staff would always get escorted off for dealing with a prisoner.

I have seen dudes fall in love with CO's and fight other prisoners behind them. I have benefitted if one of my peoples was dealing with one. That's how I came to drink E & J brandy for the first time.

The compromising of female staff is a way of life in prison. What did a man have to lose? I didn't mess with them. I also know of a few CO's who were in relationships with dudes who were fucking males. Prison is definitely crazy.

I knew my journey in these mountains was coming to an end. The new parole rumor was you had to get to the lowest prison level you can, in order to make parole. I was going on 14 years all done on maximum security prisons. At my annual review hearing my prison level dropped to medium security.

I keep my routine until I was transferred. If there were any ripples, it was dealing with a lot of fraud Five Percenters. I didn't mind the ones who turned into gang members. I knew this lifestyle wasn't for everyone. Some didn't want to leave the criminal mentality alone and refine their thinking. I knew that people weren't living by the street or personal codes any longer. I would have been a fool carrying a dying flag.

It was Jive Pretenders[52] who use to come to an established cipher and try to influence it with their weak knowledge and/or

---

[52] A term reserved for fake Five Percenters.

behavior. I had a large hand establishing the current cipher. The core cadre was discipline, well-read, respectful, respected, and militant. I didn't sambo step for the administration. They labeled me as one of the leaders, which was laughable to me. I knew they didn't understand our tenets at all.

I watched Jive Pretenders become more frequent. One lame on his first day on the camp from coming back to prison was pushing teachings counter to ours. I asked him a few degrees. He knew none of them. They were the ones he could have used in his weak argument. He didn't even know his Student Enrollment[53]. I was diplomatic with him and helped him renew his history. In the Five Percenter culture that means to get his Lessons back memorize and go study. He just kept on being fake and divisive. We had a saying understanding comes in time. He thought he was tough based on his physique. I dismissed his antics because he was young, still growing, and from a rural part of Virginia. I knew from having a personal conversation with him his life experiences were limited. He started poaching weak Five Percenters and created their own cipher. It was their right. He even picked up a student and named him Wizard. That was funny.

One of the characters he had with him was a coward. He had asked me about another Jive Pretender who fell into the homosexual game. I had history with the brother before he turned gay. Even squashing some beef for him when I just met him. He was still trying to teach our teachings. When I was asked about him, I gave up his history. The coward ran back and told him about our conversation and added some shit, because the dude was cell partners with his brother. When the gay dude saw me, he looked offended, and asked did I say what he heard. I am thinking to myself I only gave up your history because you are not one of us. I didn't feel like picking and choosing about what I said or didn't say. I was like yeah. I said it all so what's next. In my mind, I knew I would never present myself like I couldn't

---

[53] Student Enrollment (1-10) were 10 basic questions and answers that every seasoned Five Percenter should know.

stand for what I said. And I was alright with whatever he wanted to do next. Which was nothing.

I was like where is the coward. He stopped coming to cipher and rec. He was the worst type of sucker there was. When I did see him, he was with the muscle-bound Jive Pretender, and his student Wizard. Muscle man was like can I build (talk) with you. I was like what's good? He started complaining how he didn't feel it was right that we had two ciphers up here. I knew why he had come back with his tail tuck between his leg. He had no knowledge. I was the one that gave him his Lessons. I said it's not two ciphers it's one, on Saturday, and open to whoever wanted to attend. He got the point. His attempt at a power grab had failed. It failed because we moved as a collective and his character was weak. **Every God was equal, but not all of us have equal ability.** At different times and situations, the better knower is giving the floor.

I started to evaluate the last few Jive Pretenders I had bumped heads with. The worst encounters I had was from the used-to-be New Yorkers, who left when they were children. They tried too hard to wear the NY banner. I was always skeptical about these fellas. If they felt their tongue wasn't as sharp as yours or didn't know as much as you; then they would oppose every thought. They set themselves up as an ideological enemy. I was into studying different political movements. I learned how factions in organizations or governments caused the downfall of them. The two greatest examples were The Black Panther Party (Huey vs. Cleaver) and Grenada in the 80's.

I felt myself betraying me at times. I wanted to attack some of them physically. That's the duality of self I struggled with. Some of them needed a swift smack in the face and kick in the ass. I lived by the code if two Five Percenters fight one must die. Our difference wasn't that serious for a death match. I still had a few things to work on about myself, but I did have it under control. I kept my mind focus on a better tomorrow without cell bars.

I thought back to when you would come on the yard, and it was hundreds of Gods and the *"Peace God"* was genuine. It always was one cipher, but in it, you had many Gods who clicked up because they had the same interests whatever it was. I knew that era was gone. I just hated that I witnessed.

I ran into plenty of brothers that was Five Percenters back then. A lot of them became ranking gang members, some went into religions, some went crazy studying esoteric sciences, and others just lost their spark. Prison kills a lot of people while they are still alive.

Nobody knows how they would react to doing time until they do it. Hard dudes on the streets become Tinkerbells, soft dudes become certified gangsters, and anybody can go crazy at any time. I think we all lose pieces of our sanity in degrees. No man does his time unscathed. It's just some of us wear a better stability mask. I guess it's the reason I feed my mind with new ideas. I was working it out keeping it strong. I didn't want my people mask to fall off.

Lunenburg

"Knowing yourself is the beginning of all wisdom." Aristotle

They called me back to the building to pack my stuff for transfer. That was always a bittersweet moment for me. I built bonds with a core cadre of good men. These brothers were my surrogated family. Since I was older than most of them by at least 7-10 years; I was their big brother. For most of them, I was the first serious man in their lives that they could share their inner thoughts with. They confided in me. I never betrayed their trust. It's a level of bonding that goes on in prison that is way more advanced than what it is in the free world. I knew I might never see some of them again. The ones I do, it will be when they have more time under their belt. My security level was finally approved for a medium.

Maybe I thought, just maybe I will make it out of here before I hit 48 years old.

Lunenburg

I was glad to be leaving out the Mountains of racist mental midgets. I was heading back to low land. I took time out to reflect on the mistakes I had made and the ways I had grown.

The two mistakes I could see vividly in my third eye was how I carried it from the beginning to the end with my Five Percenter lifestyle and socio-political views on life. I stayed in one element mode—fire. I didn't try to practice earth, wind, or water. I knew I still had a high disdain for the police and racist. I had to let it be known it was no fear in my heart. It was too many cowards on that plantation. Things could have turned against me up there. But in the end, all people respect men, even racist CO's. I never saw them having power over me. I always viewed my situation as one of compromise. In reality, prison can't run without it.

The second mistake I made was getting into petty mental wars with Jive Pretenders. I didn't realize it to later that people who have no shine will oppose you to imitate yours. People outside looking in think both are shining on the same level. They don't know the other person is a moon just reflecting the light of the sun. I learned people un/conscious do this as a power grab strategy.

I realized you can't really know yourself until you are faced with challenges and obstacles. I am who I am based on the accumulated choices and experiences I gained from them. I still was a work in progress; a duality of self. I had a vision of the man I wanted to be, but could I fully be that man in here. I struggled at times with keeping the monster in me concealed. I am a rational thinker and knew a win, and momentary satisfaction is still a loss. I was shackled and chained to another prisoner, so my journey through Beelzebub's Heaven continued.

Riding on a bus for hours is hypnotizing all you see is country. They take the scenic route just in case you have the resources to pull off an escape. I don't remember any successful escapes from prison. Even the ones who did escape was captured quickly. When you are resource poor, your chances of being successful on the run decreases by negative numbers. I never saw the need for them to take all these detours like we were going to the Lost City of Atlantis.

I did wonder how long my journey was going to last behind steel doors. I never cursed the codes of the streets I just knew they weren't for me no more. I wished I could say I regretted what I was locked up for, but I wasn't. I moved on what I understood to be true at that time. And every situation is not black or white. In life, shit happens. Either you stand-up or fold. Every man has a choice. It's easy to accept happiness but hard to accept pain and discomfort.

On solemn moments, I always thought about what I could have done differently. When I pinpointed that one person got multiple people indicted. It bonded to my memory like a bad trauma. Only one conclusion played in my head. I guessed it was the inbred code in me that surge through my body that betrayal warranted death. I knew I was never going to see that coward again because the court system had rewarded him nicely. He was already out the system for at least 6 or 7 years.

I ran across people that was cool with the other snitch. The story he spun on why he was incarcerated was because of computer fraud. I thought to myself these cats don't check paperwork. It was very rarely I or somebody in my cipher didn't know what a person was locked for that wanted to be around us. The funny thing was this yellow back had hooked up with a Mobb Deep affiliated that was doing time down here. When he got out, he was in dude video. That was insulting seeing this clown in a video masquerading like he was some authentic person. I knew no more protocols of the streets were being applied. I was glad I tapped out young.

The first thing you want to do after a long bus ride is stretch your legs, but you can't because you shackled to another human. The little things about being incarcerated is it's always a reminder of your fallen status. I wondered how going from a one-man cell to a dorm of a 100 people was going to be mentally for me. Some people like being around a lot of people, not me.

All intake routines were the same. Only the faces change. Another new intake was like *"Peace Allah"*. He saw what tray of food they brought me and heard my name. I had legally changed my name even though, I was named after my father; who I respected. But I was not a white man from Britain, so I shouldn't carry an English slave owner name. I was a member of the Five Percenters, and it is customary we change our names, but we don't have to do it legally. I just chose too. I was a larva coming in as one thing, being transformed by an iron cocoon, and I was going to exit as something more exotic. A Black man with knowledge of self, a transformed mentality, and a different outlook on life. It was a poem called Two James by Nikki Giovanni that I read when I was in the receiving center. It resonated with me. I would remember this stanza in it that said, *"from cells, you were born, and from iron cells, you will be reborn."*

I knew my journey was going to be different but how different I didn't know. I was in for a cultural shock. When I went to my dorm, it was a warehouse with about 100 beds. I knew from a quick view this place was probably designed to hold half that. I went from the silence and solitude of a single cell to a madhouse. Living in a cell environment for almost 14 years to this. I question myself am I going to make it.

My qigong practice was going to be needed. I was uncomfortable my first few nights. Any sane person would think about his safety in this open environment. People also had a bad habit of walking through the bunk aisle instead of the aisle design for that. When I asked, a few people don't do that when I am resting, they got offended. I knew why they were just doing what was customary there.

When I observed, a little more and start talking to people, I realized that most of them either just came in the system or only been on level two(s). I rationalized they didn't know any better. All the men who did were the ones that were coming down from higher levels, trying to make parole like me. I knew I was going to have to suck it up and figure out a way to be in the building less as possible.

They literally had nothing to do if you had a GED, HS diploma, and a trade already. This place was truly a warehouse for the despair. I had to design a meditation/qigong routine and study other techniques as well. I had to find quiet time to study or design a new way; that was easy. I just zoned out the noisemakers by playing my jazz cd by Paul Taylor. His saxophone kept me focused. I had to get a job that kept me out the building for a large part of the day. I knew I could be a tutor, but when I went to applied, I was told that you had to work cell house or in the kitchen first before you can get another job.

I thought to myself this sound like some bullshit. I applied for the kitchen, anything to get out the building for a while. I chose the afternoon shift, dudes avoid it because you have to deal with lunch and dinner chow. The times I needed to be out the building. Since I got up early, I was able to read and go to first rec called to work out. That shift worked out perfect for me. I took the job nobody wanted which was pots and pans. You work all day, nobody bothers you, and dudes avoided it like the plague. The other fellas that work the line only work the line doing feeding time. The staff expected them to stay busy the whole time. I thought that was funny. The young ones would try to duck and hide. I am thinking to myself that is too much work. I stayed busy on pots and pans and if I had a work partner our shift went quicker.

Being in my 30's gave me a different understanding of things I would have frowned upon years ago. One thing was the gunning culture. [54] I realized in an abnormal environment strange habits develop. But doing that in the kitchen peeking out behind racks was on the creepy side. I remember when I was around 22yrs old and an older brother who I was cool with, told me a story how they caught another inmate fucking the meat. He was like we beat his ass. I could imagine.

The average free person doesn't realize how incarceration deteriorates some prisoners' minds. I always took the time to school the younger ones, especially who had small bids to do. I knew that was my duty to drop a jewel on them. It's always been a class of honorable men in prison, and it always will be. I was just continuing the tradition.

One afternoon some little dark-skinned man popped up with the kitchen supervisor and was like *"come with me."* I was like who are you. He kept repeating himself. The kitchen supervisor smirked. Because I am questioning a person that is telling me to come with him, but he never identified himself. At times, I am on my Brooklyn bullshit. We went back and forth for a few minutes. Then the kitchen supervisor was like he the investigator. I am like to myself *"what the fuck do he want?"* I basically just got here. He is standing there like that supposed to mean something to me.

---

[54] Prisoners that choose to masturbate off the female C.O.s without their permission.

As we leave the kitchen, he said, *"you are not in trouble."* That's when I paused and said, *"I can never be in trouble only children get in trouble."* I figured I set the tone early. A habit I carried with me from my youth. He was looking at me crazy, and I couldn't understand why. You a man like I am. We just in opposite positions. I didn't stop carrying my core values of manhood. As we walked to his office during chow call the boulevard was packed with people going to the eat. My peoples saw me. They were concerned. In prison when the investigator come get you, it's never a good look. It usually ends with you being put in some type of disadvantage position.

When we get to his office, his partner was there. A super plus size sister. She came off to me a bit slow. I was informed that in a few minutes an NYPD detective would be calling to speak to me. Now I held my cards close. I was wondering why. I automatically assume they are fishing about some murders or somebody implicate my name in something to get themselves off. Now I am in full gangster mode. I never know anything, so I knew this is going to be a waste of a call. If they were charging me with something, then I would have already been served with paper.

I understood that some weak fellas relish for calls like this for they can turn into a rat and get out of doing the rest of their time. It's various reason dudes betray their own honor. They rationalize it's to get back to their family, or their crew didn't hold them down like they were supposed to. It wasn't any shelf life to this gangster shit. All you could do is transform your thinking and maintain the base of a stand-up man. And ratting is never in the equation.

When the detective called, he was placed on the speakerphone. He started out on the wrong foot trying to fish on who I knew back home. Of course, I didn't know anybody. I asked him what precinct and division he was from. When he told me, my tone switched to insolent and fuck you. I reminded him I don't sell drugs, been locked up for 14 years, so I have no friends on the street. And don't never contact me again because I am never going to know anything. But I said all this in my MD the Dream persona. It's funny how easy it was me to switch from Mallah-Divine to that mask.

The look on the investigators faced was shocked. I read their minds. It was like he just talked to an NYPD detective like he wasn't shit. I never viewed people in cop suits no more than enemies. I would never be used as a tool to make a cop's case.

I went back to my dorm. I deducted who the detective was trying to see who I knew. The precinct gave it away. I knew I couldn't send a letter or use the phone to inform him he was hot. I gave them enough credit that they would monitor my outgoing mail and phone calls. So, I sat for like two months before I pushed a letter to make contact. I never knew if he got it. I don't know if he was even alive. He was a state to state hustler. That is what he knew and wasn't trying to change. I met a few people like him on my journey. They love the lifestyle. They didn't want to change the criminal mentality. They thought the next time was going to be their big money run.

I adjusted to the dorm lifestyle as much as I could. It wasn't my type of bidding. The level of seriousness was low and too much circus and bread.[55]That is never a good thing. I carved out my space and did what I do. I continued reading, studying, working out, and engaging like minds. I did talk to the young dudes because they were interesting. And started to understand how popping pills, smoking weed, drinking cough syrup, and liquor at the same time had messed them up.

Once I moved into the position of a teacher's aide helping them get their GED I really understood how chemically unbalance they were. They lack discipline, focus, and would throw fits like a child. I knew they had been prayed on by an arch deceiver. I just couldn't prove it. But I studied enough to know that it's to the powerbrokers benefit in America to weaken every generation of the Black male. If you can't critically think you pose no threat and a brute can be caged. The more I worked with them my theory was being validated.

---

[55] Sport and playing

This was the first generation in my opinion who really looked to rappers as heroes. They got mis-educated through thrash music, drugs, and negative images. I could not help but to think about the CIA's MK Ultra program[56]. If you study the consolidation of media in the hands of a few white men, you will see how the quality of music being promoting went down. It was a conscious effort to show the Black male in the worst light possible to the world. When you control the narrative to what people see you control the ideas the feed off.

In the class, it was young dudes to old men striving to get their GED especially when VADOC made it mandatory. One time I had to check a clown. I just had became his tutor. He kept giving me an attitude like I was some sucker or Uncle Tom because I was a teacher's aide. He wasn't a young dude. I expected better from him. I could tell he never did time nowhere but on this kiddie camp. I didn't let it slide either. I bent over and whispered in his ear, *"If you got a problem with me we can step outside and handle it."* He looked up at me, grabbed his workbooks, and went to the table with the white aide. The most precious commodity you have in prison is respect. And it's not to be negotiated. The funny thing he was happy like a puppy for the white dude. I dismissed him as another self-hating Negro coon. It's a disease when Negros view another Blackman as their enemy. But turned their booty up in the air to be fucked by the white man. This breed of coward always disgusted me.

The lady I worked for was a typical white liberal. She reminded me of a colonial missionary. She always thought she knew better. And at times her behavior and words were condescending. When the younger students picked up on it, they would flare up. I always deescalated the situation. I knew if they hit that old lady, the staff, and then the court system would make an example of them. I had their respect and attention because I always gave them my best. I was genuine with them. Plus, I would give them my ear if we were in the dorm area or on the yard.

---

[56] Mind control program.

She didn't realize or cared that she treated the white aide different. She saw him as a grandchild or something. He did his best to keep his nose in her ass. She acted like he was smarter than us because of his upper-middle-class upbringing. I used to think he wasn't shit. He tried to put a hit on his own parents. I used to laugh because I knew the other aides' backgrounds and none of them were slouches. One was a cryptologist in the navy and college education, two others including myself had some type of formal education, and all was well read.

She stayed overestimating his ability. We (aides') taught the lesson to our tables and at times taught a class. When it came time to give class lessons when it was math she always gave to him. She used to want me to teach the calculate, which most people don't know how to use. My young partner was an aide too. He used to laugh and was like you getting away with murder. I used to tell him when people assume on your ability or lack of it you let them. I always was in strategic thinking mode. It was a skill set I developed early. When people saw you as just a thug, hoodlum, or gangster; because of the way you speak or rough demeanor, you let them. I learned that in middle school. Just because if you violate and I might smack the shit out of you, didn't mean I didn't know trigonometry.

White privilege breeds a disease of arrogance that her pet manifested during Black history month. Since he was an artist, he did a piece for the Black History contest on the symbols that were on quilts during the American Slavery Period. He was sharing his work with the class. He kept referring to the African symbols and people as 'slaves' when talking about their heritage. I kept looking at the Black student's faces and how they were sinking in their seats lower and lower as he said kept saying, "slave this slave that." I corrected him. I said those are not slaves' symbols and it didn't come from slave culture. He was like yes it did. We both read the same book. It was the teachers. I said those symbols came from different ethnic African cultures. He was like they were slaves. I was like no. The different African ethnic groups didn't become slaves until they came to America. They brought the symbols from their culture with them. Which they weaved into quits as a secret language of direction for the underground railroad.

I saw the students started to sit back up in their chairs with pride, especially once he conceded. In the following classes, he didn't say slave symbols or culture. The teacher was like do I have one aide jealous of another smirking. I looked at her like she was a damn fool. The weakness of some white people is they think; they know your history better than you. I considered my personal political ideology as Black Nationalist Pan-Africanism. I started studying the global African experience at 19yrs. I studied it from a historical, socio-political, and cultural angle. People must realize when they out their league and lay down or get embarrassed.

When I went to give my demonstration. I did it on Haiti and on how Western powers keep the country weak. As well as how America occupied Haiti twice. She immediately challenged my information and the source. One source I had was the Slingshot Newspaper. She questioned their credibility because it was not a mainstream source. I went to the computer pulled up the encyclopedia and showed her. She had a dumb look on her face, and I continued teaching on my subject.

I never talk about things that I don't know or unsure of. I don't give people an opportunity to poke holes in what I am teaching.

The teacher took a special interest in me. I felt like she thought I needed saving and watered down. I was too Black. She started to bring me books on people stories like the Jews like their plight was comparable to Black people. Yes, the Holocaust was a European tragedy, but it was nothing in comparison the transatlantic mass murder of African people. I used to read these different books just to discuss the ideas with her. Once I realized she didn't even read most of the books, I would skim through them and talk about those parts.

She didn't realize I knew more about other people's history then most people knew about Black Americans. I think her missionary personality of I'm saving this monkey got in the way of her seeing my level of intelligence. It far exceeded her limited understanding of me. She figured if I can make him assimilate he will be a better person. I was already a better person. The point she missed because her intentions were fraudulent.

I was always cordial with her. She always viewed most of us aides with a crooked eye. Always assuming we were scheming. But with the Caucasian aide she would deal with him like family. It didn't go unnoticed that no matter how long we worked for her we still were niggers and prisoners. Therefore, we were up to no good. It showed the oxymoron in her dealings with me. I expected no less from her.

One day she assumed I was doing something other than my job. She went on a tirade. I wasn't in the mode for that bullshit. I held my hand up and told her to *"be still and let me speak."* She was shocked, and the whole class got silence. I said it in a tone like shut the fuck up. While I had her frozen, I explained what was going on. She looked dumb again. I thought about quitting, but that was just my ego. I realized that I enjoy working with people and helping them either get their GED or just increase their knowledge base.

After class one of my walking partners was like I thought you were gone because of the look on her face. Then we both started laughing. He knew I didn't give a fuck. I would never let anyone make me into a slave or take a position of a lesser man for crumbs.

One of the things in prison that I despised was how some prisoners begged and pleaded to keep their jobs. When you witness this, you lose respect for a man. The two things you have in here is your character and word. Once you compromise one, you compromise them both. The one thing I pledged my word to was I came into prison as a stand-up man, and that's how I am walking out of here.

Living on LCC

"When someone betrays you,
it is a reflection of their character, not yours."
Unknown

I am on the yard one day and my name ring on the loud-speaker to go back to the dorm. When I get in it's the investigator wanted to see me. I am thinking again. When I got into the counselor's office, they wanted to take my picture like the police do when you first get arrested. I was like what is this is for. They are like you going into the gang database because you are a Five Percenter. I knew for years the tides were changing ever since the NY Bloods started to get a stronger foothold. When the gang label started effecting Five Percenters more and more, I knew I couldn't stand on the sideline any longer. I had more legal knowledge and skills than before when I filed the first lawsuit.

I called a Universal Cipher and had a discussion with the Gods on the next move we should make. We agreed that we would file a 1983 legal challenge. We all agree to chip in to pay the 350 dollars to file it, and I would lead it. The Gods Original Thought and Sword would help me do the legal work. I already had sent for the Jail House Legal Manual which was a great weapon to aid in this battle.

As we progressed with the legal fight. I was called to the investigator's office again. This time they had switch them. This one was a Caucasian. When I got there, he had the head gang unit investigator with him. A Negro yellow-back from NYC, some clown back in the day we would send to the store for beers. I respected them both as much as I respected spit on a pig. I knew these fleas would try to annoy me. I already had my indifference mask on.

They asked about me challenging the responses I got for being turned down for a Nation of Gods and Earths class. When you start a lawsuit, you have to build your paperwork up showing that the VADOC is systematically hindering and putting an unnecessary burden on you from practicing your way of life.

They sat back in a cocky position. I felt it was unfair that I had to dialogue with these mental midgets. The Caucasian one came out blatantly and stated, *"I got all this gang stuff started against the NGE."* I smirked. I expected no less from the Devil. That irritated him. He felt like that was supposed to arouse me. It had no more effect than a gnat flying on my skin. I saw this was going to be a bait game to see if I explode. That way they can send me to the hole for threatening an officer. That would reclassify my security level, get me off the compound, and send me to a higher security level. It would remove me momentarily from my battle team.

The Negro lieutenant jumped in, went on how he was from NYC, and been to the Allah School in Harlem. I asked he why you are down with mislabeling us a gang when you knew better. He started talking some bullshit that didn't make any sense. We were going in circles. I knew about him. He was just a regular CO before the East Coast Bloods started saturating the VADOC. He sold the VADOC that he was some type of gang expert. He weaseled his way in having his own unit. They would become a gang with their own symbol and colors. I Hated weak mutha-fuckers like him that swam in lies, drown others, just to come up. I had a silent rage for his type. I smiled at the thought of just whopping his ass.

They both sat back snug like they had the better hand. They did because it was equipped with falsehoods. The Caucasian said, *"You know you in the bible belt."* I was like thank you and got up indicating this meeting was over. I never let lesser men dismiss me. That made him hot. As I was walking out. He stood up and said, *"Don't think we don't know you are filing a case"* He said that with a snarling look on his face like checkmate. We knew your move. That just validated my point that they were stupid. If you had an informant amongst the Five Percenters, why blow your strategic advantage. I just looked at him like so what and kept it pushing.

I wasn't going to figure out who his spy was. I called my trusted cadre, shared the information with them, and the measures we were going to put in place. It was no more updates about the legal battle at our monthly Parliaments. We also kept all the legal work and strategy between us.

I knew to be a state informant is the lowest you can go. Informants trade their brothers trust and forfeit their personal honor. In my eyes, their penalty should be death. In honorable cultures, especially the ones that live by Warrior's Creed it's totally acceptable. But we live in America where rats and men of no integrity are looked at as heroes. Sometimes I felt like I was born a few centuries too late.

Bloods

"I had to laugh at young brother tried to recruit me.
He said I would make you a 5 star under me.
I said I outrank your OG I am God." Mallah Divine

My dealings with the different Blood factions was interesting. Most of them were younger than me and from NY/NJ. I had ran into two that were my peers. They were from different sets: one West Coast the other East Coast.

The one from the West Coast set we did time on a different compound earlier in my bid. He wasn't Blood. We weren't associates then. We used to have some spirited discussion. He used to be a follower of Dr.York[57]. He still read his books and study some magic information from some old texts. He thought he was going to build his skill up by speaking some unknown language and call these demons to be under his command. I just listened. I thought nothing of it. I had seen plenty of people lose their minds dealing with magical esoteric sciences.

He was a crook at heart and mind. It was no transformation in him going on. He asked me a question of what I think of the Blood thing. I said you have too many weak members that can't stand on their own. If I was into that. I would immediately kick out all the weak ones, trim it down to a core unit. Then I would carry it like the Mafia with made-men and everybody else auditioning to get a shot. I would only select the best of the best. He just looked at me rubbing his chin.

It was just simple math and marketing. If you make something exclusive, people work harder to get in and respect it more. He wasn't a boss but a foot soldier. I never understood how grown men could put themselves under children leadership. I liked him. He was a good dude, but reckless.

---

[57] Dwight D. York, also known as Malachi Z. York, Issa Al Haadi Al Mahdi, Dr. York he founded different movements.

My other peer that was an East Coast Blood claiming he was a 3-Star General. He was from NY. We used to talk a lot. He was on his second bid and a used to be Five Percenter. He knew a few Gods I knew. All the information I needed to do a background check within my network. He wasn't a prolific builder in the Nation of Gods and Earths, probably why he was a Blood. Plus, he liked to sell drugs.

Our talks weren't as intellectual or spirited as with the Blood from the West Coast set. It was like I was talking to a child and not my peer. He liked that he was followed by young dudes.

One morning one of the Gods and I was working out on the small yard attached to the building doing our Qi-gong and stretching exercises. We would do that to the next gate break then go work out with weights on the big yard. One of the other Gods pulled up to the fence told us an incident had happened on the weight pile with two 85ers[58], and one of the other Gods got involved because that was his man from the street.

I saw the God and the 85er walking the track. I called him over. He told me what went down. Some Bloods tried to jump his man on the weight pile over some weights. You would be surprised how common this story was. He was like I got this, this not Nation business. He was serious, and I respected that.

He was one of the stronger stand-up Gods I would meet. When the gates opened, we walked over to where the crowd was forming. When the other Gods saw us, they stopped what they were doing, and took up strategic positions. But we were seriously outnumbered by the different Blood faction. I assumed they would all pull together and a few of them had gone in to get bangers. All we had in our favor was brotherhood, heart, and we would go hard for each other.

When the 3-star General came out, he was like what's going on. The dude in question wasn't Blood, but his cousin was. I was like that's the God's man all he wanted was a fair one. He doesn't want his man jumped. And if he gets in it, I can't let you jump him. So, let them other two dudes square off like men. The dude

---

[58] A non-Five Percenter.

cousin was like it *"ain't no fare one."* I am looking at these little dudes, and all I see is fear in their face. I see the God's man rushing at them and them little dudes running backward. I am watching the God and the other Gods watching me. Because if he jump in, we all in.

The whole time I am thinking this is some bullshit. This is what happens when you put children on the compound with men. The CO in the tower grew tired of seeing the little dudes run sprints, so he called it in. CO's came from everywhere locking down the yard. I knew what was coming next.

I started seeing dudes trying to stash their bangers. The tower CO's with their binoculars were watching it all. There were also cameras on the yard. As we were getting pat down to go back in the building the CO's in the tower were calling people out on the walkie-talkie. They were escorting them off in handcuffs.

When I got back inside the General came to my bunk area, sat down, and asked me how he should have handled it. I told him you did a poor job of leading. You rode with a cat who wasn't Blood and started the whole situation. He should have fought the fair one. That is why your organization grows weaker because nobody is ever tested to see what type of man they are. He just nodded his head in agreement. I always felt the street organizations didn't realize their potential to be change agents. But the people in authority did. It made for an interesting zero tolerant dynamic towards them.

I knew the prison authorities would come for him. The VADOC knew all the leadership and people associated with it. No Gods went to the hole because all we were doing was observing at that point. The man that wanted the fair one went to the hole, but he would get out a few days later. The gang members would go on to a higher level. If the loudmouth and his cousin would have stood their ground jumped him, and the God jumped in, then this story would have had a different ending. They were no neutrality in the thick of things. That's why it was important to associate with men with nothing to prove. So, if it does go down you alright with the fallout.

When dealing with the Bloods, I always had to keep in mind that most of their OGs and first wave of them use to be Five Percenters or heavily influenced by us. You could tell that in the language they use. Some sets even borrowed our Supreme Mathematics. One little brother who I let read the *Knowledge of Self*[59](KOS) book came to me one day while I was at a table studying. He sat down and said I have to show you something. I was like alright. He left and came back with a folder of Blood literature and the KOS book. He pulled out a paper in his folder. Part of their teaching, they had borrowed a Plus Lesson from the Five Percenters called the 7 Characters of a Wiseman[60]. Then he went to the KOS to show me like I didn't know. He started to question his allegiance to them. He was a young man who had gone from juvenile to an adult prison. I just listened to him without any input. This was a choice he was going to have to make on his own. But it just gave me more ammo to what I already assumed about the formation of the NYC Bloods.

One day the highest-ranking leader of a Blood set in the whole state of Virginia was like, *"Yo the new guy that be with you is a snitch. It's a red light on him."* I lost a little respect for him right then and there. He didn't have any black and white[61] nor saw black and white. He took a statement like that on face value. I was fully aware who was around me. I was educating this brother to our teachings. He had *"black and white,"* it spelled out who was snitching. It wasn't him. But the fact that this was a rumor I knew I had to jump in front of it. I told the Blood his information was inaccurate according to paperwork. He knew the rat was just trying to cover his tracks. If the rat never tried to spread a false rumor, the Bloods would have never known the truth. The younger brother wasn't looking to oust him. He was

---

[59] KOS in an anthology of Five Percenter's writing.
[60] A Plus Lesson credit to First Born Prince.
[61] Black and White is legal paperwork.

more hurt by the betray, especially from someone he got a lawyer for. In the end, I knew cowards do what cowards do.

A God and I had seen a group of Bloods on the yard, and we approach them. We asked what their thoughts were on this red light? They were like we heard but that's not our business. I was like why not? They were like we Westside. I still let them know the black and white told a different tale. I was always keen of the different politics that exist amongst the Blood factions.

VADOC was getting more aggressive with their gang unit. Doing things like having the whole dorm strip down to their boxers and stand in front of their bunks. They would go down the aisles and inspect each one of us like cattle looking for perceived gang tattoos (real or imaginary). It's not what they did but how they use to do it. They showed more gang behavior than the gang members. All they was doing was bullshit. They were just trying to justify creating that unit. The more nonsense they made up, the more funds they would get. They would eat at the expensive of a lie.

I used to talk one of the young gang leaders about moving wise. He used to do this elaborate Blood handshake and make a noise in front of the CO's. I used to remind him G's move in silence. He was like I don't give a fuck. I am a certified gang member from the streets. I am already in the database. These the times that passages from the *Art of War* would pop into my mind. In this case, it was *"know your terrain."*

I found him to be a good dude but a poor leader. Especially to be the highest-ranking Blood from his set in the whole state. I also question the sanity of his OG that gave him that rank. A good soldier doesn't always make a good general. I would see that too often within the gang's leadership structure. They had some of the poorest skilled people in the most apex positions.

I got to know the poor leader more. It validated my first thought even further of him being a good dude. We never talked about street shit. We did talk about his children and running a dog kennel when he got out. He was on the downward swing of his time. I encouraged him to learn all he can. He went back to school for a trade which he took extremely seriously. He liked to build with me on Christianity. I saw hope for him, but I knew it would be short-lived. He loved the gang lifestyle and was an intricate part of his national organization. I didn't judge him. I knew he had to negotiate the best path for himself.

One day him and his whole set got sent to the hole. That was not out the ordinary. I figured the VADOC would use them to pad their stats for they can justify more gang money.

His captain came out the hole and dropped his flag. My spidey sense went up. I never saw them let anyone with rank back out. He started to be enlightened by one of the Gods from his town. I knew more about gang protocol. I asked him how he went about getting out. He claimed he had his leader blessing. That was his right-hand man, so it was feasible to me. But I always thought this brother was weak. I took no position on his transition. He attacked his studies viciously. He soaked up knowledge and brought his own books to deepen his under-standing. I started to warm up to him, then the other shoe dropped.

His educator had sent word to me that it was extremely important. I stepped out at door break. He was already on the fence waiting for me. When he finished giving the rundown on what had really happened with the Blood leader and the flag dropper. I said call a Universal Cipher for the 6 pm door break. I told him I going to build with the Gods in my building.

At 6 pm we had a Universal Cipher and put the culprit in the middle of it. We started to interrogate him about what really happened to his leader. We also had a smuggled news clip from the local paper. The VADOC didn't let that day's paper come in, and I see why. It stated that the gang leader was being charged with multiple conspiracies to commit murder and looking at a possible 625 years.

We probed this potential turncoat. We asked him if you were his right-hand and the only person left from that set that was still on the compound, why is that? He lied. Another God asked why do they keep calling you to the investigator office with the local Detectives? He tried to play tough and was too defensive. I am thinking he played a hand in this brother downfall, who was 90 days from going home.

In my mind, it was no definitive proof that he was a rat, but I knew he was. He was the go-between the gang leader and the orders that got send out. It's impossible for him not to get indicted unless he was snitching. I remembered how he moved with the Bloods. He liked being a gangster. He used to love his role as the underboss. Just to give all that up for no reason was always fishy to me. The Gods were split on how to move forward. I was like I am not fucking with him. A few of the Gods who had done the same amount of time as I felt the same way. We have been through too much to take a chance to get bit by a snake. Our experiences required us to take the nuclear option and live with the consequences.

I always thought back to what an old head told me when I first starting bidding, *"There ain't no secrets in the penitentiary."*

The word came down through a kite to one of the Gods from the gang leader detailing what happened and the role the flag dropper was playing. It was still an ongoing investigation. When he was pressed by the God that was educating him, he came clean. He was using his mother to forward the letters to the other members. Which was dumb because the VADOC monitor active gang members mail. They knew all the lingo because other weak suckers been revealed that. In exchange for his mother and him not being charged, he became a cooperating witness against his leader and friend. Honor codes were surely poor in a whole breed of people. After that, the other Gods who gave him the benefit of the doubt stripped him of his 120 and turned their backs on him.

What the rat was trying to do was take refuge in our house, putting us in a possible war situation. The VADOC transferred him. He went to another plantation got down with a West Coast Blood set and took on a different name. I thought to myself a coward constantly dies to keep reinventing himself. I wouldn't be surprised if he not dead. His former leader and friend had to cop out to 9 years rather than stand trial in a one-horse town and face 625 years.

The last young Blood that would have an impact on me in memory was from a cleaner set. I had asked him what did that mean? He was saying a lot of information that was floating as Blood information in VA wasn't right. He was home team, Brownsville all the way. I gave him some insight on the last Blood who caused ripples by blasting dudes that had fake stain (rank). I let him know you still from NYC they are not going to be favorable to what you bring. He was like whatever we can get busy then. I thought to myself, *"Brooklyn to the fullest."* He was waiting for rec to go to their meeting. I knew he wasn't going to be on this plantation long.

He said something to me when we started talking about having no family in VA. He was down here by himself. He also expressed an interested in learning more about the Black Panther Party. I had a book called *Survival Pending Revolution.* When he went to rec call to handle his business. I went to his bunk area to put the book on his bed. I saw he had nothing: no TV, radio, or hygiene. I am like damn a lot of Bloods don't be having anything to be comfortable in prison or the bare necessities. I went back to my area, put a care package together for him and slide it in his locker.

When he came back in, we just talked about more progressive things. It couldn't have been 2 to 3 days later, and he was gone. Vanished. It was like he was never here. I felt sorry for him. He had been in the gang since he was 12 years old, done what he was told, sent places, but was living like a pauper. He still was giving the gang his best even at the expense of his own child.

The thing that stood out to me the most about the Bloods was their line discipline and the abuse that came along with it. I knew I couldn't be a soldier and listen to a person I saw as weak. I liked their talk on brotherhood and the Black Panther Party(BPP) as the birth of the organization, but 99% didn't know anything about the BPP. I knew when they developed to a level of having a political ideology and moved out on it; they were going to be a force to reckon with.

The tides started to change.

"I constantly retrospected and introspected, because yesterday's missed opportunities make for today's greatest lesson. I was just getting tired of applying them in prison."
Mallah-Divine

After my 8th or 9th parole turndown, I concluded that I would have to bring my whole time to the door. Even though the politics were slowly shifting in Virginia. But you still had fellas with drug and robberies conviction locked up. If it was an option to give parole to them, they would make it before people like me with a murder conviction. I prided myself on being a realist. I just accepted my fate.

I was a news junkie. I stayed up on local, national, and global politics. But something still gnawed at me like I was missing something.

I was in my mid 30's so the bullshit that moved most people didn't move me. I wasn't getting high (I used to smoke a lot of weed) or gambled. I didn't mess with homos or play sports. I didn't run a store box or sell drugs. These are the things that put you in confrontational situations. I have been taking the stance that the parole board would just have to keep using their rubber stamp and turning me down for the **serious nature of the crime**.

By this time, I was burned out with prison. All I could do is keep my mind sharp and body right. I was practical. I didn't get into the esoteric sciences or ancient spiritual philosophies. I stopped wasting money and time on the UCC-1/strawman information. I knew when I was released I had to have an action plan. I developed an agenda ladder. It consisted of a ring of circles from smallest to largest.

I started with creating a circular diagram, writing me in the smallest circles and then writing one word on each following circle. The closest circles to me are the things I needed to do immediately based on my ability. The first one had family because building my ties back with them was essential.

After I had something on each circle, I would take each goal and do the same technique making it more targeted. You can think of them as dart boards. The reason I called it the agenda ladder is because if you viewed it from a different angle, it could be seen as a ladder to reach the top. I would make columns (goal, skills have, skills needed). I would do this every year I went up for parole. The concept behind the way I designed it was I didn't set an agenda based on time-limited. I did it based on resource, abilities, and skill sets I had or would have to gain.

I even had an emigration plan. It was no way I was going to do 28 to 32 years in prison and stay over here in America barely making it. That was my last move, if I had to execute it. I figured I work two years and just stack money and then leave. I had a few African countries in mind.

I had seen so many people proudly come back to prison it was a shame. I was walking to chow one day and seen a fella I did time with a decade earlier. He was just getting back. He recognized me and was like *"Yo you ain't been home yet. I have been home twice."* I was like Nah and kept it pushing. I was thinking to myself he liked to fuck homos so being in prison was heaven to him. He was a petty criminal type. While to me prison was *Dante Inferno*.

I concentrated on the legal battle I had initiated against the VADOC. I would see the depths they would go to lie, to keep this gang label on us. They claimed it was 5000 members of the Nation of Gods and Earths, but they only had 3 recorded incidents involving Gods. And those incidents spanned over a 10-year period. One was a group of Gods training on the yard. It's ok if you run basketball tournaments but not workout together as a unit. I am like this is bullshit. The real reason they didn't want us to have legitimacy was we teach the Blackman is God. We advocate self-responsibility, knowing who you are historically, and culturally. They knew we had the keys to transform the criminal mind to something much great.

The officials want you to be religious zombies. They knew it was a sedative. Religion makes the average person weak, hoping for a better place in the next life. I had seen many people detached themselves from reality and all they did was read religious books. I didn't knock them I just felt sorry for them. It's like they believed in magic. I saw no difference in that and children believing in the tooth fairy. I figured to each his own.

I focused on the better tomorrow. I wouldn't be detoured by other distraction. Fighting the case on behave of the Nation of Gods and Earths kept my spirit alive. When you start reading legal cases you come to understand how unfair the American society is. They really have a problem with Black people not identifying themselves by the standards or ideas that they set. This what makes a Five Percenter a threat.

I knew we could win. It was an uphill battle based on the deceitful ones had resources and lies on their side. The God Original Thought and I would spend hours in evening law library session. Besides us working out together and walking miles around the track, this really solidified our bond. I learned most people just talk support, but few will roll up their selves and get in the trenches with you. It reminded me of a statement I heard Malcolm X had said, *"Who wants freedom? You have to start by killing the 200 people who didn't raise their hand..."* My take away from that is your own people will hinder you in your cause by just standing on the sideline.

Just living in a dorm brings a lot of challenges to you. I never had privacy. One time I am watching CNN and a brother come over was like, *"Yo that white dude just moved in the dorm was on the news for killing that Black football star."* I was like why the fuck you are telling me for? I was like the young dude that got killed have family and friends that are on this camp. That's their business. That case was interesting because he got 10 years for shooting up a car with an AK that had a 100-round drum on it. The young football star was in the car with a Caucasian girl one of the shooters old flame. The local Blacks protested the minimal sentences that were given. But in these country areas, the judges look out for Caucasians. I witness it too many times.

I was posted up talking to a fellow thinking and overheard the little Caucasian bragging to a booty bandit predatorial Negro on how the AK was spitting at the car. The booty bandit and me caught eyes. He knew I disapproved. But I knew his angle and what the result was going to be for the shooter. He was going to get what his ancestors had done to mines called buck breaking.

The next day it was raining and only a few people were outside. I just finished working out with Original Thought. I spotted the little Caucasian and told him to come here. I saw that he was nervous. I stayed seated while I talked to him. Mainly because he wasn't a threat to me. And psychological he had to know this while I chastised him for feeling comfortable enough to tell that shooting story. When I dismissed him, he had a better understanding of do's and don'ts. I did it because I knew if one of the young dudes heard him bragging and hurt him. They would have caught a new case. It was a handful of young dudes I was cool with. I wanted to see all of them go home on time.

Nobody but us knew that discussion had taken place. I never like to handle things around a bunch of eyes. That was a carryover trait from my youth. On a one on one basis you can see what a man is made of. A lot of beefs get stirred up because of the other eyes watching, which fuels some people foolish pride. I never liked confrontation. I just didn't know how to shy away from it once it was initiated. I learned a lot from disappointment and lost. I learned diplomacy is a better skill to have. I practiced it a lot maturing in Beelzebub's Heaven. If my generation had learned this skill set at an early age, it would have saved a lot of useless bloodsheds, wakes, and prison bids.

It was like living the same day every day. Then a fight happens especially when wine is available. I used to drink it from time to time when I was on a higher level because I was in a cell. In a dorm, it's no privacy and wine give off a noticeable odor. This wine was not Malbec or Merlot.

It wasn't any wine on this compound in years. The few that tried to make it got knocked off because of the smell. You couldn't burn incense because smoking was banned. But when it did hit it was comedy central amongst the young dudes. They didn't know the art of just being still and enjoying yourself. They would get rowdy. Someone would talk too much shit and invite an opponent to the bathroom. It reminded me of that old movie *Mad Max* When they put you in the terror dome to fight for your life. The queen would say, *"Two men enter one man leave."*

One man always left and usually the inviter be bloody and knocked out. The CO usually picked up on the change in the dorm's natural flow. What happened next is routine. A squadron of CO's come line us up like animals and look at our hands for bruised knuckles. You must have a strong mind not to allow these practices to dehumanize you. I just grew indifferent to it. It usually was a Friday. When I was done being inspected, I went back to watching the Sci-fi channel. One of the few indulges I had.

A lot of these young dudes were at the beginning of their bids. Some wanted to make a rep for themselves others just wanting to do their time and go home. When these views collided, somebody was going to lose face, and both paths would be altered. I was glad I started my bid on higher levels because it was a serious atmosphere. Where violence could lead to death because a lot of prisoners were never going home. The only commodity a person had was respect, and that was worth killing for. So, these dorms are viewed as kiddie camps to most seasoned bidders. It doesn't make the danger less real. It's just a less intense environment. Who wanted to be brought into a kangaroo court getting another charge for a fight? On that compound that is what they started to do if you broke a person's skin. The charge would not be assault but malicious wounding.

The thing that shocked me the most with these young dudes was when the heroin showed up. They would flock to that shit. I expected it from the old heads, most of them were trapped in the Blaxploitation Era. It had surprised me that it was so many young dope fiends. It was a sad sight to see, but always educational. You can't count on no dope fiend. If I had seen anybody that I associated with caught up in that whirlwind, I would have cut them off. You must maintain your personally standard at all cost. We still in prison. I never forgot that.

I could tell when the mood changed something was about to happen or has happened. The drug that brings misery and death was working its magic once again. The little fella that had shot the Black kid with the AK had OD like 3 am. His team of knuckleheads was scurrying around. One was giving him CPR. All you felt was the stillness of death. The floor officer that night was a female, and she didn't know what to do. Another prisoner had to calm her down and take charge. He went to the booth officer and had him call medical. It's always a coin toss if they were going to make it to you in time.

I sat on my bunk thinking that this little dude was having a traumatic prison experience. He had got fucked by predators. If he was a racist, I knew it had to mess his mind up that black males had repeatedly penetrated him. When he started turning blue, it looked like he was going to lose his life. I had seen many people overdose in my life it was nothing for me.

When medical final came, I heard someone whisper behind me he, *"dead."* All I knew was we going on lockdown, and an investigation had started. I didn't care if he was dead or not. When you play with that drug, you sign up for the risk of dying. I remembered when I was young, and people would die from overdosing in my hood. They called that dope the smoker. The package was intentionally sent out strong for it to kill somebody. The fiends ran to it. Whatever you into you should stand the consequence even if it meant death.

He didn't die. His whole team got removed after urine tests and camera footage. The one thing I never forget is that we have surveillance on us all day everywhere. It was a fact of life. We were lab mice. At times, the administration would go overboard. If they saw any group size gathering not associated with some sports foolishness. They would call the investigator, and he would post at the fence with the binoculars. The guards in the tower would be walking with their rifles out. Everything was a show of power from these mental midgets' standpoint.

I was getting tired of prison. Now and then the top echelon staff would make their rounds in the slave quarter. The inmates would run to them with their complaints. They didn't figure it out that these people created the policy they were complaining about. The CO's was just enforcing them. I knew for sure that these fellas were broken. They were no longer free men in the mind. When you think your adversary is going to treat you fairly, you have gone insane.

I have been on compounds where I heard inmates say, *"He likes me,"* referring to either a CO or top staff member. In my mind, I used to be like that slave needs to be killed. That is the mentality that thwarted the Denmark Vesey and Gabriel Prosser revolutions. I couldn't help but to make comparisons between the characteristic of prison and slavery.

One day when the top staff came in and was walking down the aisle. I stopped one and asked her, *"why do you'll come in here like overseers?"* She just looked at me, but when I finished explaining my point her facial expression agreed. One of the young dudes had seen the exchange. He said, *"MD I knew you were going to say something crazy."* We laughed then I explained, *"you can't see them as having power over you. You just lived a lifestyle, and this is the flip coin to it. But you don't become a lesser person, and you should never let lesser people every think they have the better of you."* He nodded in understanding and agreement.

My eleven-parole hearing was coming up. It always fell a week after my birthday. I would be 39yrs old. The process was robotic to me now. It came to a point where your hearing was conducted through a tv screen. My family did what they always do write letters of support. My mother had a phone interview with a member of the parole board. In Virginia, you don't see the parole board you see a parole representative that sends them a written report. Then the members vote on it. If you get 3 out of 5, you go home.

My mother was feeling different after this parole interview. They had asked her more probing question on the support the family would give me. I let her be my mother and kept my thoughts silent. In my mind, I thought realistic I had 2 to 4 more years to do before I look like a candidate for parole. I based it on the average time those that were making parole with the same type of charges as me. They had pulled at least 21yrs and better.

On my parole day, they almost forgot to call me. That wasn't a good sign to me. It still surprised me the level of incompetence of some of these CO's. Why I referred to them as mental midgets. I got my pass and walked over to the hole to go talk to the TV.

As I was heading over there, I had seen one of my oldest allies. He was coming back with great news, he had made parole. I felt like I made it. He was down since 17yrs old and we were the same age. He was strong physically and mentally. He had been preparing like a madman for years for a shot at the free world. He had successfully dealt with transforming his criminal mentality into a progressive one. I knew he would go home and win.

I went into the building that housed the hole. They placed me in one of the visiting cells. I can see it's like five or six people ahead of me. My building was going to the commissary. I was like damn I am going to miss it. In my mind commissary was more important than going up for parole.

As I am waiting, I see a prisoner wrapping a square block on his head and rope around his arm. I took him to be a converted Jew that was a thing amongst a portion of Caucasian prisoners. Some didn't want to be Christians or embrace the Odin religion, which was supposed to be the Viking's religion. A few converted to Sunni Islam, most of them were fake and moved like snakes to me. People must believe in something greater than themselves when they didn't understand themselves. I didn't knock where sincere people sought strength in order keep them going.

I kept thinking like damn this shit going too slow. I am definitely going to miss commissary. I had no magic key to unlock the minds of those judging my worthiness for freedom. I did what I was supposed to by submitting a parole package with my letters of support and accomplishments.

I heard the key in the door. I knew it was show time. I went swaggering into the room where they held the hearing. There she was in the corner of a 32-inch monitor. I also wonder why her image didn't take up the whole screen. I sat down in my usual seat. She asked me was I still studying the import/export business. I was. She never asked me did I have remorse for my crime. This was my third time seeing her, and it was my shortest interview. She just literally looked at me with compassion on her face. She knew, and I knew it was no more I could have done in prison. I was the ideal parole candidate. I had not caught an infraction in 13 years. My vocational slot was filled up. I was a teacher's aide. And still had strong family support.

After a brief silence, I excused myself to leave. She really did have compassion on her face. She told me as I was leaving, *"I am giving you a good review."* That was the third time I heard that. I knew she meant it, but she didn't have a vote in the process. I always thought that was crazy. How is the person interviewing me don't have a vote?

The whole parole process was political. This is how criminal minded thugs turn progressive in their politics by being politicized through the process. As the VADOC tries to dehuman-ize you, it has the opposite effect on a few. They become aware through their empirical experiences by getting hung on the barb wire of the injustice system. I was no different. This process tried to suck the hope out of me and shatter my fortitude. My resolve turned into titanium. I had no hope of making parole. I concluded that a long time ago, but I still stayed prepared. It was the student in me. It allowed me to have the intellectual tools to rationalize my situation.

I was a captured dragon but the fire in my belly still burned. When I return to the dorm, my cut partner was like how it went? He was new to prison and under the no parole law. I felt sorry for this fella. He tried his hand at the drug game late in life. He was a working man who had got injured in an accident that supposed to net him over a million dollars. Him not knowing better and being vindictive to his ex-wife turned power of attorney over to his lawyer. After the dust settled, he got 20 something grand.

He allowed me to look over his paperwork to see if it was anything he could do. All I said was why would you turn over power attorney to a white man. He knew what I mean. We in the South and white men has never shown themselves to be our ally. Especially to no dumb Negro. I was like damn. Yes, your ex-wife would have got a piece, but you would have been a few hundred thousand dollars strong. His expression told the rest of the tale. He reminded me of an old cartoon when the person turned in a donkey.

He made a lot of mistakes. He was telling everybody about this money coming. The predatorial leeches would swim around him. He would borrow commissary from different people. I gave him the game, but he chose to ignore it. His tiny fortune made him prison rich.

He was a good dude. But I knew he wasn't going to make it 12 years in here, not like he was currently moving. He was the catalyst for me writing an urban street fiction. I was currently writing urban sci-fi short stories. He used to buy nothing but urban street novels. I would always ask him to let me see them. I would read the back cover and then look at a few pages. Then toss it back on his bunk. He was like you always do that. I was like this shit is trash. It was like all the story plots was the same. A few of his books were put together technically poor. I had reviewed one that had no paragraph intents or breaks. It was like a 200-page prose.

A lot of people use to come to our cut area to borrow his fictional thrash. I didn't like it because our privacy was already limited. I did see how many people like reading those types of books. I thought to myself that is a way to educate the people. It would be like sneaking castor oil in orange juice. I came up with the concept of writing urban political street thrillers. As I wrote I let him read it.

He was like are you going to get this publish while you in here. I was like no. A lot of publishers of that genre were robbing people; giving them like 500 dollars for a manuscript. I rather let my work die than to be cheated. Money never moved me. I wasn't going to mortgage my self-worth for it.

I continue to work on it and my short sci-fi stories. Writing was my refuge. I would play my Paul Taylor cd and zone out. I could write for hours in the worlds I was creating. The visuals I would see when writing was so vivid in my mind it was like I was there. I had transplanted my soul to paper. This was the strongest creative outlet I had. It was saving my life, but I didn't know it. By creating emotions for different characters, it was allowing human traits in me to stay alive. My pen was the conduit to trapped sentiment. Writing wasn't a hustle for me it was a lifeline to sanity. I was pouring my essence into my creation, fashioning new worlds, and loved it.

I thought back, what if that teacher never kicked me out of my 8th-grade creative writing class. Every element in my life was interwoven. I was a tapestry of good and bad experiences. I had a reservoir of water to share. The only blind spot was would I be able to share my creation with the masses. But for the moment it was my dingy in a sea of chaos.

A few months had passed since I went up for parole. A few more fellas made it. I thought to myself that billion-dollar prison budget is starting to take its toll on the state coffers. The prisoners with no parole started that hope talk about bringing parole back. I knew that wasn't going to happen as long as it was a few thousand people eligible for parole. I didn't get into those discussions anymore. I realized men must have optimism in something to survive. That was keeping them strong to make it back to their families. I was matured enough to know I didn't need to win that debate.

I came out the shower getting myself ready for chow call, and my name gets called over the loudspeaker. The counselor had wanted me. My cut partner was like they have been calling your name all day. I thought to myself these mental midgets still can't get it right. I never saw the purpose of signing out the dorm to go to wherever you had to go if they never checked the log book.

I was like it's nothing but that parole turndown I will get on my way to chow. I kept getting myself ready to go eat.

My counselor was out, so I had to see the other one. When I get in her office, all I see is a stack of parole turn downs. When she handed me mine, I was condition to go straight to the back page to see the reason why for the turndown. When I got there, I didn't see it. I looked twice then I went back to the front to read it. You have been granted release on parole. At that moment, my eyes looked up and was magnetically drawn to hers. She just smiled and stated, *"You know you left a lot of time, please don't mess this up."* I just shook my head in acknowledgment because I was leaving 10-15 years at their door.

What I was feeling was a cross between joy and bewilderment. I just had turned 39 and realistic thinking I wouldn't get out before 44. But here I was at the gates of triumph. I felt like a general leading his troops in a victory parade. I thought back to that moment when I was in the hole at 26. I told myself if you want to get out of here before 48 you have to be more strategic with how you move. You don't have to show your disgust for the authority openly. **Know your terrain.** It was at that point where I had created another mask for myself to wear. It was called nothing. I gave nothing. I showed nothing. I became unreadable to them. Their harassment tactics was about effective as an amoeba would have been to an elephant. I started seeing them for who they were: mental midgets. I knew they couldn't out think me. It was a few thorough CO's that wasn't about that harassment bullshit. If you carried it like a man, they dealt with you like a man.

I knew what the next phrase was. I was going into their reentry program for six months. That meant I would have to move to the others side of the yard. Change was hitting us all. The God Original Thought was going to the FEDS to give them 12 more years. A few other Gods was maxing out in a few months. We knew the legal case we had was good, but my name was on it as the only plaintiff. Once I walked out those gates, they are going to dismiss it as moot because those Constitutional violations wouldn't affect me anymore. It was a battle we stood a good chance of winning. I wonder did that play a factor in me making parole as well. I was one of the few progressive Five Percenters left that was from a certain era.

I had seen the technology change in here from a Walkman to a CD player to a digital tablet. I wouldn't be getting one. I started to understand how prisoners was a captured market and a goldmine for companies like Jpay. On higher levels where CDs were now banned because you can make a weapon out of them (I never saw one), you can only purchase tablets. New prisoners could only buy tablets. Jpay was already selling music and on some compounds movies. I knew it was time for me to go. I could do no more on this realm.

Last days

"America is the land of the second chance - and when the gates of the prison open, the path ahead should lead to a better life."
George W Bush

I packed my property to move to the building across the yard. It was nicknamed the Go Home Building. A lot of people was genuinely happy I was getting paroled. But others had the sour puss look on their face. The strong greetings of peace from some turned into weak what's up or head nods. I didn't really give a fuck. We all played our hand. Only thing I was apprehensive about was somebody stepping out of line, and I had to defend myself. I would more than likely lose parole.

The reentry building was an interesting experience. It was programming you to reenter society by forcing you to take around five different programs. I had to go to the gym in the morning where a meeting would take place. That was supposed to get you used to being up in the morning conditioning to be work ready. It was some bullshit. The resistance to the programming was understandable. It didn't do anything.

Most men already knew what they were going to do when they return to their respective hoods. I was no different. I had a skeleton blueprint already mapped out. I was getting antsy to leave. I had been in the South too long. I was ready for the NY smog. I had condition my mind to expect nothing and take my time. I just had to finish these programs. I didn't complain about them. I went through them because they were obstacles to my liberty.

Once I finished them a memo came down from the director of the program that you had to do the full six months in the program. That infuriated me. I didn't even need the programs to begin with because the resources where Virginia based. Other fellas who had made parole and completed the programs were released before the six months. I was done in July but had to wait to September to leave these hell hold. I would finally do hard time.

I did what I always did when I get agitated, create a mask to cope. It was better for me to hide my dissatisfaction than to be disgruntled. It wasn't a thing I could do. I stayed in bid mode until it was my time to exit Beelzebub's Heaven.

I used to watch the nervousness in fellas, reality had set in, and most of them pissed their bid away. **They didn't prepare—** it always reminded me of the Aesop Fable the *Ant and the Grasshopper*. I had remixed it and used to tell it. It was true. I considered myself the ant. I prepared for my day to be released, even though I didn't know when it was going to be before my mandatory. I just knew I had to stay sane, healthy, and unbroken when I left here. I did my best to keep some of my humanity. It may sound strange, but you grow disconnected to a lot of things that keep you human in here. A place with no babies and women to offset a purely male environment. There was nothing to anchor you to an emotional base.

I went through the motion and kept my eyes on the prize: September 10. I had told myself when I was a younger prisoner I didn't want to be the greatest or strongest anything in here. I was only going to be the stand-up man that I was. I had seen a lot of prisoners lose themselves trying to build a rep. Whether it was the greatest hustler, gangster, or some type of super religious person. It didn't mean shit in here. I wanted to be great in society. My name was good out there. Prison was all some people had and being important in here was all they had to live for. That was never my way of thinking.

I kept my routine of writing, working out, and walking on the yard. I interacted with people I was close with that made parole as well or was maxing out their time under the Truth and Sentence Law[62] Everybody had their skeleton blueprint of what their agendas were. We also knew we were going to have to be each other support system. When you form bonds with brothers it doesn't stop once you hit the gate. These brothers are my family, some even tighter than my own blood relatives. That dynamic is lost on the policymakers, who try to control how prisoners associate.

Every crew is not a gang, and every gang member is not crew. Men earn their respect and loyalty to each other based on their action. The bonds built are family. At our core, we are social people. That doesn't stop when you come through the back door of prison.

I used to talk to other people as well. I started to realize how time can affect a person mind based on the input they take in or just put too much into daydreaming. I never shitted on a person parade. I would just listen and only ask questions to seek more insight into their thought process. I used to think to myself these brothers needed to be released. I hope they make it based on the conversations we were having.

I was too real to waste time dreaming about being the richest man in the world. I drew up my plans to be as practical, productive, and progressive as I can. I knew if I advance

---

[62] Is Better known as the 85 percent law.

righteously my quality of life would improve along with it. My ability to make other things happen would increase as well. I knew my potential, but it was all kinetic as I stared at the ceiling of the dorm.

I learned nobody cares what you are going to say you going to do, because it's viewed as pipe dream. They want to see what you are going to do. I knew my caliber of man. In my clan, our favorite saying was *"Failure is not an option."* I had giving the state of Virginia all my twenties and almost all my thirties. I wasn't afraid to take calculate risks and play the slow, long, hand. I knew what high risk-taking had gotten me. I wasn't insane and had no desire to live by street codes no more. I had jumped off that ride and was waiting to execute my strategy. I didn't have anything to lose. My way of thinking was I could be going home in 2025 instead of September 10, 2014. I had no problem taking the slow route to my destination. I will be doing it as a semi-free man.

The one thing that stood out to me in this go home dorm were the fights. They were frequent than a regular dorm. I attributed to dude's nervousness. I could not wait to blow this noodle joint. I used to get that question are you nervous about going home because you been down a long time. My answer was always the same **I can't wait to get out of here**. I used to remind people this is abnormal. We supposed to be free. I figured that most of these brothers weren't who they were portraying to be in here out there in the free world. I guess we all wear masks. We take on personas that is needed to survive.

Another thing I was waiting on to get approved was my Interstate Compact to New York. I was going home. Once that was set in stone, the fire of anxiousness started to flare up. I wonder what NYC looked like. I still had contacts back home, so people shared stories with me. I used to read the New York Amsterdam Newspaper; it was the oldest African-American newspaper in the country. I was familiar with the gentrification taking place in theory. Prison had taught me to be more aware of the socio-political landscape of any place I'm going to be ten toes down on.

One-person other than my immediate family knew I was coming home. Most people thought I was buried in a shallow grave. They associated my 55 to life bid with New York time, which would have meant I would have to do the 55 years before I started going up for parole. I was written off by many like a bad debt. It was an old saying you can't keep a true G down. I was about to prove it right.

My last 30 days

I always took a rec call to walk by myself and reflect. I knew it was almost show time. That was my most enjoyable moments. I was calm and seeing clear. I had finished my manuscript for my first book. My living conditions were settled. I had 700 dollars in my account to go home with. It wasn't much, but I figured I could at least buy myself some work clothes. My family was excited. I knew that was my strongest resource. A lot of returning citizens didn't have that. I knew I was fortunate in that area.

I thought about the humiliation I had to endure. I thought about all the shit I had let slide. I thought about my co-defendants the ones who were snitches and did a fraction of the time I did. I didn't have animosity against them, but a part of me still wanted to blow their heads off. It's nothing worse than traitors. I thought about my other co-defendant who had got sent to a higher security prison for an infraction. We were in the same boat. I knew his chances of making parole was setback. He was a warrior I needed on the street. I trusted him explicitly. Our bond was forged in the fire. I never heard a bad word about. He made his way and remained a stand-up man.

I thought about my other co-defendant who didn't rat but took a plea deal after being on the run for 5yrs. I held the most contempt for him because we grew up together in Bushwick. We were also co-defendants in another case in NYC from our stick-up kid days. We were like Frick and Frack. We were inseparable.

Most people thought he was my cousin or brother. I had held him down without ever blinking an eye or any regards for my personal safety. Even during this case, I was offered a time cut to tell his whereabouts. When he was on the run, I always got kites from him and occasionally got a number to call. When he finally got jammed, I sent him my transcripts to make the best move for himself. He took a plead. He did his 6yrs and never was heard from again. He forgot what true brotherhood was based on: **Loyalty and Reciprocity**. The code is you always stay right to men that spilled blood for you and with you. He turned his back on me, and that was worse than snitching. His character flaw surfaced. It was selfishness. I thought about all the time I wasted with him. I thought about all the danger I got in because of his rash behavior. I lived by the code if we family I'm holding you down at all cost. He manifested at the end he only lived by it when it benefited him. He taught me my greatest lesson.

I analyzed my past 19 1/2 years. I dissected it like I had the latest surgical tools. The people I once knew. Who had stayed true and who didn't. What I had lost for *"KEEPING IT REAL!"* The good brothers I would be leaving behind. And what I had gained as I traveled through Beelzebub's Heaven.

I unpacked all these thoughts as I walked miles around the track. I knew I was going home as a respectable man without a tarnished name. I knew if your name was good and honor in tack, doors would open. I knew I could look myself in the mirror and recognize a man. I never folded on anything or betrayed anyone. I followed the codes of the streets. I was not taking those garbage values home with me. I knew what it could do. One fella I did time with, went home and cut a female head off. I knew it was personally mixed with some street business by the nature of the brutality. He never talked that violent talk. Every time I saw him on the yard, I would interrupt him from listening to Keith Sweat to build with him. He was one of the few older homeboys I had that I dealt with. I had a good idea what harboring negative thoughts could produce in a person if they felt like you violated the loyalty rule.

I knew I wasn't MD the Dream no more. He had burnt to ashes, and Mallah-Divine Mallah had risen from them.

The Day

My last evening rec call. I hung out on the yard with the Gods I was close to. I didn't have to tell them bullshit like I am going to get at you with I am released. These brothers were my family. I made sure they got first picks at my property that they wanted, which was mainly the books. These brothers were happy that one of their own was getting out. I knew word is bond not as a statement but a core pillar of being a man.

When rec call was over, I went in and broke bread with my cut buddy who was leaving weeks after me. We always had good discussion. His mind was dead set on going out there and being a good father to his children. I admired that. I knew he would succeed. He was one of the few people I heard that had their children as the motivating factor in all the other moves and choices they wanted to make.

When I went to rest, I felt like a kid on Christmas eve. I couldn't wait for the next morning to come. I tried to watch TV until I got tired. It wasn't working. I felt no jitters. I started to feel like I am really going home. I had the mentality that it's never real until you walk out the gate. As the seconds ticked on the clock getting closer to the rooster's crow, I was feeling vigorous. I managed to get some rest. I was up before the lights in the dorm came on, but that was my normal time of getting up.

I did my Qigong for the last time in a prison setting. I knew the routine. It was going to be count, breakfast, rec/school call; and then I would be called. The loudspeaker crackled *"Mallah-Divine Mallah."* It was show time. All cameras are on me. I felt like a movie star. I had the red-carpet strut.

I had to go to property to get my clothes. I wasn't leaving in no state clothes. This form of slavery was over for me. Per my request my people had got me black everything. I was leaving like a smooth ninja. When I put those clothes on, they felt different from the state clothes. Maybe it was my mind.

I had to turn in all my state clothes to laundry. I was one shirt short. Now, this guy was an extra special asshole on every laundry day and today was no different. We got into an argument because he wanted me to go back to the building and find a shirt to turn in. I wasn't going back to get any state shirt. As he kept talking, I felt the urged to smack the shit out of him. He was a special type of Negro. The female property office saw what was going on and called me over and told me don't worry about him. Then she dropped a piece of info on me. She was like he the one driving you to the bus stop. I shook my head in disbelief.

My family wanted to pick me up. I veto that action. I thought for a second, I should have let them. But I wanted to take the bus home and just experience a free me again.

All my paperwork was signed off on. I strutted down the boulevard in all black about to blow this cuckoo nest. On both sides of the yards, people were saluting me. I felt like General Hannibal riding on an elephant in victory when he crossed the Alps and defeated the Roman. I came into Rome and didn't do what Romanians did. I didn't fold. I didn't indulge in homo activity. I didn't let my mind get institutionalized. My spirit wasn't broken. I never bowed down.

Every step I took the prison frost was dripping off me. This would be my first time walking out the front door of a prison since 1994. That was the last time I saw my brother on a visit at Auburn Prison. From 1995 to 2009, I only had entered prisons through the back gate. Just like in the Jim Crow Era our people had to go through back doors to be served.

Once I reached the main building, I started to feel the mask loosen up. My walk had an extra bounce to it. My Bushwick swagger was slowly reintegrating itself into my nervous system. The lady came and brought me a debit card that had my money on it. I was buying my own ticket since I was leaving Virginia. They would only provide a bus ticket within their state boundary. I was following the North Star. The only down point was I had to wait for the laundry man to come to drive me instead of a CO because they were short staff.

As I waited, everybody behavior towards me changed. It was more pleasant. What a difference crossing over a threshold make. I felt like I was in the final episode of the *Twilight Zone*. But I still was on prison ground, then my driver came.

Once I stepped through that door walking to the truck, it was an urge in me just to yell *"I am still standing!"* All the humiliation I had to endure from mental midgets. All the dark thoughts I had to let filter out my body. All the times I held my tongue because it didn't further my aim. The only goal I had since reaching 26yrs old was getting out before 49yrs old without compromising myself. I had done it.

I walked out as one of the unbroken!

Refinement in Motion

"Very few people in prison have voices that go beyond the wall. It's my job to do the work for them because they have no one."
Mumia Abu-Jamal

My thought process for writing this book was I didn't want to write a memoir. I just wanted to contribute my essay to a larger project. When I saw it wasn't going to happen, I turned it into a memoir. That's when the healing process came to me. Every thought I shared or didn't share was restoring my humanity and allowing me to reflect on what I really had been through. I had no blueprint or model of success to study of a person coming home from doing 19 1/2 years in prison. All I know was I am not going back to Beelzebub's Heaven.

I have to constantly negotiate the best position for myself. I exist on a razor blade edge and a slip off will have me going back to prison. I realized I was not free as long as I am still legally obligated to my sentence. I was aware of it, but I didn't let it handcuff my mind. I knew I had a bigger task like reconnecting with my family which is a work in process. Who I was yesterday only exist as a shadow in their minds. I knew I had to show them through my activities and behavior who I am today. That I lived by a different creed, applying another level of discipline. That my mental was refined through hard times, so I understand different. I knew in time all this would reveal like a slow leak.

I evaluated how family and friends dealt with me. I knew how I had played it was right. I didn't let everyone know I was home at the same time. Everyone that I did see or reached out to it was all love. Some of them I could tell didn't know how I was going to respond to them. Most people had written me off. They thought the next time they saw me, it was going to be in the next lifetime. But here I am. What I had realized early in my bid is a man must make some journeys in his life alone. That is when he grows the most.

My family situation was stable. It was a bit awkward for me at first because my father had past when I was inside. My mother was remarried, and it was a different energy in the home. It wasn't what I remembered, but nothing stands still in life. I knew when you add or take an element out of an environment it changes. My father was gone. I acknowledged that but too actually feel the lack of his presence was something surreal to me. I had robbed him of his last days to interact with his son because choices I made. The impact was hitting me in small doses as I reintegrate myself into this new household.

When I left, my mother was fairly a young woman at 39yrs old. One thing that had not change is how we interacted. I loved that familiarity. I used to always talk to my mother in the morning in the kitchen while she made breakfast. We continue that. She is genuine happy I am home. She is the only person that never second-guessed me. When I told her, I was going to publish a book and go back to school she knew I was going to do it. She knew I would find a way to execute my plan. I took that vote of confidence and ran with it.

Once I knew my mother and me was solid, I had to repair the one with my little sister. She went through a lot. She was 15 years old when I left. The death of our father came when she was 18th years old. She was daddy's little girl. Then compound that lost with both her brothers locked up in two different states. I couldn't fathom what she had been through without no men supporting and protecting her. As we talked, she would tell me things a little at a time. I would internally take it in and wonder does she resent me. She would always say, *"You wasn't here."* I could not help but feel a little guilt. I was so into being a stand-up dude in the streets that I forgot to be one in my house. I had dropped the ball. I didn't realize or consider the magnitude my absence had on her. We in a better space now. We had always been tight; it's a Capricorn left-handed thing.

I reestablished my family bonds. I also had to create some with those that were babies when I got locked up. As well as the ones that were born during my incarceration. Those are works in progress. I am a stranger to them. That's a funny feeling being a stranger in your own family. I am glad I am getting to know them.

One of my little cousins had passed away since I had been home. He was the one I would always get as a toddler. He was five when I left and twenty-five when I saw him again. Soon as he saw me at my other cousin going away party, he busts out crying with overjoy saying, *"My big cuz is home."* That made me feel good. I thought he wouldn't remember me. Seeing him two years later in ICU ripped the scabs off my eye ducts. I turned my back and let the tears roll unfiltered. All I thought about is my lost moments with him.

The greatest advice I had gotten when I came home was from one of my OGs who I highly respected. He had done ten years in prison and been home for more than a decade. He told me *"Don't deal with your PO like you dealing with a CO, go in there and talk. Let them see what is going on with, and what you are trying to do."* I took that advice to heart and did exactly that. He was telling me you not in war mode no more. You have to transform into a civilian mind state. That advice got me months away from being released on early parole.

Some of you might think you already a civilian, maybe or may not. But the context and standpoint most people like me come from are different. The mentality that I carried was unlike the everyday 9 to 5 folks. It allowed me to move in currents that at times was dangerous. I never acknowledge that brand *"I am a real nigga"* or *"Street nigga"* or *"Gangsta."* I was just me. I came out of my house and was going to be the best me. Sometimes that included breaking laws other times it was holding myself down in tight situations or standing with friends in their time of adversity.

I moved out on the understanding I had at the time. In life, it's a universal principle that states what doesn't grows dies. I grew and still am growing. I became a mature man in prison. I am living and embracing manhood on more than a few acres of fenced in land. Showing and proving I can live without being confined like an animal. I am doing a pretty good job out here. Once I left prison, I never thought about being there again.

I love the man that I have become. In my time home I have faced a few challenges that tried my patience. When dealing with people with poor behavior, it pushed buttons that make me switched to a dangerous mode of thinking. When that happens, I just keep calm and do my breathing exercises, and a tranquil vibe comes over me. I understand even in a win it is a loss for me. I figured to be underestimated is the greatest feeling in the world. This must be how the mongoose feels when facing a cobra.

I lost a few job opportunities at critical times. That's when I dug a little deeper and didn't let self-doubt creep in. It can kill your progress and let you see other moves that are illusions. I keep my focus, following the blueprint that I designed for myself. I made adjustments as needed.

I self-published my first book **The Hidden Hand: Duality of Self** with limited resources and know how. But I learned. The internet is a great tool coupled with a lot of companies that provided what I needed to execute my independent spirit. I didn't move the units I felt I should have. But I got more out of it as an accomplishment and a networking tool. I was able to sit on my first career panel as an author for Safe Space. An organization that deals with youth. I was formerly incarcerated and sitting up here with a nurse, college professor, national guard recruiters, and director of a nonprofit.

Since I do not hide the fact I was in prison. Someone asked me, *"what was the greatest resource a person could have coming home?"* I had said *"family."* I was lucky to have it. I could see the different struggles others had who didn't have a family as a resource. As I shared my story with these young people it became therapeutic for me and a lesson for them.

I accepted that I am held responsible for detouring some of the youth away from the hells of prison. Where ever I am at I take a moment to stop what I am doing to either listen to them or share my experiences. When it's nice outside, I would grab a table and write on my laptop in the middle of the projects. By default, I am giving younger people a different look. I didn't worry about people thinking I am soft. I knew people being naturally curiosity would do their own research on who I was. In time I would built a respectable bond with a few of them. It came in handle one day because I was able to talk one out of doing something that would of send him away for a long time. I think when young men share with you in their moments of turmoil that's when you are obligated to give them the best advice.

I knew building equity in my character was essential and becoming a community stakeholder. I am a **credible messenger** when it comes to dealing with youth that were connected to the street or already court involved. I also learned that in a society that paperwork is respected. It doesn't matter if it's certification, degrees, ownership, or fiat currency. I embarked on a journey to go back to school at 40 years old. I graduated with a Computer Network Technology AAS (and working on a BA in Computer Systems).

I knew I had to become as community stakeholder as well. I was able to do that by helping in a basketball tournament that was organized by the Nation of Gods and Earths. I got involved in social justice issues and advocacy that centered around the prison industrial complex like the ***CLOSErikers Campaign*** and ***The Millions for Prisoners Human Rights March***. I was able to help in the organizing phases, speaking on panels, townhalls meetings, and even had an opportunity to go to Albany, NY to lobby for the ***Kalief Browder Bill***. The most rewarding thing I had done was help built a playground sponsored by **KABOOM!** in one day for the children in my community. It is an honor to be an asset.

The one thing that stands out about being on parole is I need a pass to travel out-of-state. It put me in the mind of the travel pass slaves needed to move at night. It reinforces to me you are not free yet. I always get them when I need them. The last time was on my first vacation. I went to Hawaii and got a chance to swim in the Pacific Ocean. Just being out there was a great experience. I had a room on the 23rd floor. My view was a volcano on one side and the Pacific Ocean on the other. Who would have thought less than 3yrs ago I was on a prison yard in Virginia? I thought about that one night while I was in a lounge chair and sipping on Remy. It inspired me to write a blog on my website called *"Thinking: From the Prison Yard to the Marriott Beach Resort."*

No matter my quasi-free status, I don't let fear or detractors stop me from accomplishing my agenda. I am always in a progressive mode of thinking and planning for a better tomorrow. I realized it was just somethings out of my control and I can't let disappointments turn into a funk. I always need to be clear minded and discipline in my approach. It's turning out to be a great experience for me using foresight rather than hindsight. I am making my own history and didn't become a recidivism statistic. I am in that percentage that the media don't mention. I consider myself Harriet Tubman I will help others navigate their way past the traps of recidivism.

If I could write and speak to people about my experience and earned a living from it, I would probably just do that. I realize you have to be a **credible messenger** when it comes to talking to the youth or anybody that wants to know a real perspective about prison and the streets. I was honored to be an Arches Mentor working with youth/young adults on probation. That was my most soul fulfilling job to date. I always take moments to give a few words of wisdom to younger brothers when their ear is available.

I know I am securing a better tomorrow by preparing now. I realize that I must be a **mentor** to those who want to walk the path of freedom. I have my ups and downs, but that's regular people sh*t. I know only those who successfully navigated a storm can tell somebody else the method they have used to get through it. I am honored to be amongst the 32.8% who never get talked about.

"When the prison doors are opened, the real dragon will fly out." - Ho Chi Min

I made the right choice to transform my criminal mentality to one of a Progressive Resourceful Thinker (PRT). I already concluded that I am too soft to go back to prison. I like drinking hot sake, eating sushi, and using wi-fi. Yes, I have a sense of humor. One of the wonders of not being on hyper-alert status in a hostile environment. My story is still unfolding stay tune...

Poem 9,984,960 Minutes

9, 984,960 Minutes (In Prison)

My life ticked a humble experience.
Humbled through humiliation in a wretched
Condition.

Blood tears and no fears, militant shift in my cerebral.
It made sense—no compromise—no surrender.

Bowing and knee jerking, praying on a dead savior
On a piece of wood. No not me. Who I am.
A true and living Good Order Direction.

My mind saturated with the wisdom of
Great men filter though the ambition of greatness.

I turned pain into an assets; despair, displeasure, and disdain
into a fuel.
I'm high octane.

I survived with the strive of a revolutionist,
Black Panther politics and God body intuition...I'm still here.

Survival Rules

1. Never show fear.
2. Never go into a two-man cell without finding out who your cell partner is first.
3. Never go to a new prison being overly friendly.
4. Observe your surroundings and identified who is who.
5. Be willing to protect your manhood with your life.
6. Never touch anything that does not belong to you.
7. Introspect and Retrospect daily.
8. Focus on the moment.
9. Always read the institutional handbook, memos, and anything they put out that affects you.
10. Never talk shit to the CO's then willing allow them to handcuff you.
11. Save all your institutions paperwork: request forms and grievances.
12. Get the Jailhouse Lawyer's Handbook. It's free
13. See and don't see.
14. Do not deal with homosexuals unless you are gay.
15. Never think everybody around you is sane.
16. Work out, it is a stress reliever.
17. Never steal from another prison. A sneak thief is a coward.
18. There are no secrets in prison. Never do anything that you don't want to come to light.
19. If you not in a gang don't join one.
20. Always study and develop your mind; do not just get caught up in only reading religious material.
21. Work on preserving your humanity.
22. Stay in contact with your love ones the best you can.

The Hidden Hand: Duality of Self

Still Available on Amazon and eBook

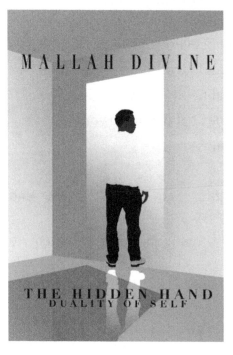

Bomani a reformed gangster just emerges back into a gentrified Bushwick with a socio-political outlook after doing 10 years in a federal prison. His former crew GBK expects him to take the underboss position. His closest friend Bo-money is the top hitman in the crew and his first cousin Max Million is the boss.

The rise of police brutality, people in the neighborhood being displaced from homes, and gang violence forces him to make some hard choices.

Bomani has other plans that have even deadlier consequences. The new age Janus wears the mask of a lover, a civil rights activist, and an urban guerrilla. He is about to launch into using strategic violence as a political tool.

Unbeknown to him he finds himself smack in the middle of battling secret societies and ancient orders. He faces a Duality of Self only question is will he survive?

Book Trailer on You Tube: https://youtu.be/K5Be27QAHy4

About the Author

Mallah-Divine Mallah is an author, writer, blogger, speaker, and youth motivator/specialist, who has published The Hidden Hand: Duality of Self. It is the first urban political street thriller. He is also a social justice advocate and worked on the CLOSErikers Campaign, The Millions for Prisoners Human Rights March, and lobbied in Albany, NY for the Kalief Browder Bill.

He uses insights from his empirical experiences that he gained inside and outside of prison. He is a credible messenger that uses his street credibility to reach urban youth striving to find their way. He uses himself as model to teach them of the pitfalls they will face by living by street codes.

He considers himself a lighthouse to guide justice-involved youth pass the pitfalls of crime, poor education, and society low expectation of them. He inspires them to see what they can potentially be once they believe in themselves.

He is available for speaking engagements and workshops. He can be contacted at:

mallahdiv@gmail.com

www.mallahdivinemallah.com

Follow him on social media.

About the Cover Artist

SAJJAD is an emerging multi-media artist based in NYC. Using a variety of techniques and mediums including stencil, collage, painting, photography and audio production, Musa's work investigates inner-city themes and expresses them in sounds and aesthetics atypical and unexpected to the inner-city culture. His collage series are socially aware and meticulously executed to highlight issues of mass consumption, connectedness, and daily life.

He can be reached at:

sajjad@sajjadworks.com

www.sajjadworks.com

Final Request

I would appreciate it if you write a review of the book on Amazon and/or Goodreads or wherever you purchased it from.

Share aspects of the book on social media that stands out to you. Join my Facebook grouped called **Mallah's Insight: books, blogs, vlogs**. I am creating a community to make the reading experience more interactive so invite your friends as well.

Share the book with your love ones that can benefit from it.

I care and appreciate all of what you are doing for me. You honor me by allowing me to share my story with you.

Thank you,

Mallah-Divine Mallah

Made in the USA
Middletown, DE
15 January 2020

83249397R00126

At 20 years old I was on trial facing life & 28 years. The John Gotti in me nev
considered losing until I heard the word guilty. I would take a soul-searchi
journey for the next 19 ½ years in prison, swimming through pain, despair, a
lies. The strive to stay human in a place of the dead was mentally, physically, a
spiritually draining. But yet I survived, challenge my former thinking, discard
street values, and developed into a man that understands his duty to the ne
generation.

"Prison Survival is his story. Mallah-Divine gives us a panoramic view of wl
goes on in the mind of a human being faced with the possibility of serving
years in prison for a murder conviction. His first-person account offe
strategies or tools for men to combat the barbaric attempts of Department
Correction personnel to break the human spirit and soul." Dr Berna
Gassaway

Prison Survival: Hell's Prism is my vulnerability, soul, and heart bei
transmitted in this book. I wrote it because I care enough to tell the truth.

Cover Art By:
SAJJAD MUSA

ISBN 9780692181614

90000
9 780692 181614